GRAMMAR WORKBOOK

TAKE CHARGE!

A Student-Centered Approach to English

JOHN CHAPMAN

McGraw-Hill

A Division of The McGraw·Hill Companies

Grammar Workbook to Accompany Take Charge! A Student-Centered Approach to English
Book Two

1 2 3 4 5 6 7 8 9 0 QPD QPD 9 0 0 9 8 7

ISBN 0-07-044359-9

Publisher: Thalia Dorwick
Sponsoring editor: Tim Stookesberry
Marketing manager: Cristene Burr
Project manager: Kamila Storr
Production supervisor: Louis Swaim
Cover designer: Vargas / Williams Design
Compositor: Christine Boyer Associates
Printer: Quebecor Press Dubuque

http://www.mhcollege.com

Contents

▼ ▼ ▼ ▼ ▼ ▼ ▼ ▼ ▼ ▼ ▼ ▼ ▼ ▼ ▼

Preface

To the Teacher

TAKE CHARGE! Grammar Workbook 2 provides simple explanations and useful practice exercises for the Grammar Check items highlighted in *Student Book 2*. This workbook is designed for in-class use, independent study, or a combination of the two. If possible, introduce each assignment in class before asking students to continue on their own.

Suggested steps for each unit:

✓ Review the boxed explanation and sample language at the top of the opening page in class. Encourage students to ask questions about anything they don't understand.

✓ Suggest that students look back at the corresponding Student Book 2 unit and go over the section in which the grammar item appears. This provides a meaningful context for the structure along with a review of associated vocabulary.

✓ Have students complete the exercises one at a time, using the Answer Key to check their answers after each one.

✓ Ask students to make note of anything they don't understand after completing the exercises and to ask about it in the next class meeting.

TAKE CHARGE! Grammar Workbook 2 introduces students to some of the most basic, high-frequency structures in English. It adds an important dimension to their language learning experience and lays the foundation for the development of increased accuracy and fluency in both spoken and written English.

Unit 1

UNIT
1

Unit 1 Grammar Check 1.1
Present Tense Statements with *to be*
• •

The verb *to be* has three forms: **am, is,** and **are.**

I	**am**	from Cuba.
You	**are**	from Russia.
He	**is**	from Brazil.
She	**is**	from Laos.
We	**are**	from Haiti.
They	**are**	from China.

A. Circle *a, b,* **or** *c.*

1. My name   a.   am   Roberto.
             (b.)   is
             c.   are

2. What   a.   am   your first name?
             b.   is
             c.   are

3. Where   a.   am   you from?
             b.   is
             c.   are

4. My address   a.   am   600 Main Street.
             b.   is
             c.   are

5. How old   a.   am   you?
             b.   is
             c.   are

6. What   a.   am   his date of birth?
             b.   is
             c.   are

7. Where   a. am   he from?
            b. is
            c. are

8. What   a. am   the children's names?
            b. is
            c. are

9. I   a. am   Chinese.
            b. is
            c. are

10. Where   a. am   she from?
            b. is
            c. are

B.   Write the word *am, is,* or *are* in the blank.

1. She   __is__   from France.

2. I   _____   Italian.

3. We   _____   Japanese.

4. They   _____   from Poland.

5. You   _____   Russian.

6. He   _____   Brazilian.

7. I   _____   from Puerto Rico.

8. They   _____   Filipino.

9. She   _____   Canadian.

10. We   _____   from India.

C.   Write *I, she, it,* or *you* in the blanks. Use each word once.

1.   __I__   am 22 years old.

2.   _____   are from Cuba.

3.   _____   is 055-33-7641.

4.   _____   is Mexican.

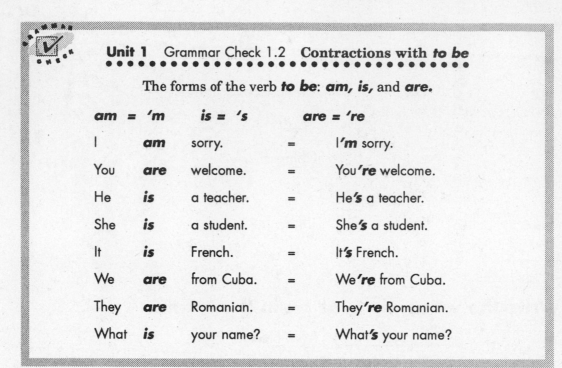

Unit 1 Grammar Check 1.2 **Contractions with *to be***

The forms of the verb ***to be***: ***am, is,*** and ***are.***

am = 'm	is = 's		are = 're
I **am** sorry.	=	I**'m** sorry.
You **are** welcome.	=	You**'re** welcome.
He **is** a teacher.	=	He**'s** a teacher.
She **is** a student.	=	She**'s** a student.
It **is** French.	=	It**'s** French.
We **are** from Cuba.	=	We**'re** from Cuba.
They **are** Romanian.	=	They**'re** Romanian.
What **is** your name?	=	What**'s** your name?

A. Circle the contractions.

My name(s)Boun Ome. I'm from Laos. I'm 34 years old. I speak Laotian and English. I'm a taxi driver. My wife is a teacher. She's from Thailand. We're glad to be in the United States.

We have two children, Orahan and Phoumy. They're good children. Orahan is eight years old. He's in school today. Phoumy's twelve years old. He's at home today.

B. **Write** *I'm, You're, He's, She's, We're,* **or** *They're* **in each blank.**

1. Roberto is my friend. <u>He's</u> from Cuba.

2. My children are at school today. _____ glad to go to school.

3. The teachers are not German. _____ American.

4. My son's name is Phoumy. _____ 12 years old.

5. My wife is from Thailand. _____ Thai.

6. I am from Laos. _____ Laotian.

7. My wife and I work every day. _____ busy.

8. It's your birthday! _____ 40 years old today.

C. **Rewrite these sentences using the short forms of** *to be.*
   (I'm, You're, He's, She's, It's, We're, or They're)

1. My telephone number is 692-0014.

   _____ <u>It's 692-0014</u> _____.

2. They are from Africa.

   _____.

3. I am from Brazil.

   _____.

4. She is a teacher.

   _____.

5. He is at school today.

   _____.

Unit 1 Grammar Check 1.3
Possessive Adjectives (*my, your, his, her, our,* and *their*)

The words **my, your, his, her, our,** and **their** come before the names of things.

These words show that a person or persons own something.

I'm Raul Rodriguez.	**My** last name is Rodriguez.
You're 20 years old.	**Your** date of birth is January 13, 1988.
I have a 10-year-old son.	**His** name is Paco.
My wife is Celia Mendez.	**Her** first name is Celia.
We have a telephone.	**Our** number is 668-3356.
Lidia and Sam live in Tucson.	**Their** apartment is big.

A.   Circle *a, b,* **or** *c.*

1. This is Alice Smith.
   a. My   first name is Alice.
   b. Your
   c. Her

2. My name is Leo Levitz.
   a. My   last name is Levitz.
   b. Our
   c. Her

3. My wife and I have three children.
   a. His   last name is also Levitz.
   b. Her
   c. Our

4. Roberto is from Cuba.
   a. His   last name is Sanchez.
   b. Our
   c. Their

5. My wife and I have one car.
        a.   My   car is very old.
        b.   Our
        c.   Your

6. You live in that apartment building.
        a.   My   apartment number is 6-F.
        b.   Our
        c.   Your

7. Son and Mei are from China.
        a.   His   first language is Chinese.
        b.   Her
        c.   Their

8. My mother lives in California.
        a.   His   phone number is (805) 555-6776.
        b.   Her
        c.   Their

B. Write *my, your, his, her, our,* **or** *their* **in the blanks.**

My first name is Oscar and ___my___ last name is Campos. I am from Mexico.
My wife is in Mexico. She is with _____ three children. The

children love _____ mother very much. But they want to see _____ father, too.

My son's name is Julio. He is twelve years old. _____ middle name is

Oscar—just like _____ name. Julio helps _____ mother with the other children.

My two daughters are Hilda and Rosa. They go to school every day. _____

school is near the house. Hilda is five years old. _____ teacher is Mrs. Campos.

C. Circle the correct word.

1. What is ((your) / you're) phone number?
2. (I'm / My) from El Salvador.
3. (He's / His) name is John.
4. (Their / They're) apartment number is 5-D.
5. (She's / Her) Chinese.

Unit 1 Grammar Check 1.4 **Question Words**

You can use **what, where,** and **how old** to ask questions.

What is your name?   My name is Javier.

Where are you from?   I'm from the Dominican Republic.

How old are you?   I'm 23 years old.

A. Match the questions with the answers.

1. What's your apartment number?   17-62 Parsons Avenue

    How old are you?   17

    What's your street address?   7-G

2. Where do you live?   Clara

    Where are you from?   Santa Clara, California

    What's her middle name?   Mexico

B. Write *What, Where,* **or** *How old* **in the blanks.**

1. A: <u>How old</u> are you?
    B: I'm 47.

2. A: _____ do you live?
    B: At 525 First Avenue.

3. A: _____ is Jose?
    B: He's 21.

4. A: _____ 's your phone number?
    B: It's 343-1758.

5. A: _____ 's his last name?
    B: It's Sanchez.

6. A: _____ are you from?
   B: Cuba.

7. A: _____ 's your book?
   B: It's at home.

8. A: _____ 's your address
   B: 790 Eleventh Avenue.

9. A: _____ 's your social security number?
   B: 075-44-9096.

10. A: _____ is Gabby?
    B: She's eleven months old.

C. Write the questions.

1. Q: <u>How old are you</u>?
   A: I'm 36 years old.

2. Q: _____?
   A: I live at 3632 Main Street.

3. Q: _____?
   A: I'm from China.

4. Q: _____?
   A: My name's Hilda.

5. Q: _____?
   A: It's 333–0400.

Answer Key

1.1

A. 1. b, 2. b, 3. c, 4. b, 5. c, 6. b, 7. b, 8. c, 9. a, 10. b

B. 1. is, 2. am, 3. are, 4. are, 5. are, 6. is, 7. am, 8. are, 9. is, 10. are

C. 1. I, 2. You, 3. It, 4. She

1.2

A. name's, I'm, I'm, I'm, She's, We're, They're, He's, Phoumy's, He's

B. 1. He's, 2. They're, 3. They're, 4. He's, 5. She's, 6. I'm, 7. We're, 8. You're

C. 1. It's 692-0014. 2. They're from Africa. 3. I'm from Brazil. 4. She's a teacher. 5. He's at school today.

1.3

A. 1. c, 2. a, 3. c, 4. a, 5. b, 6. c, 7. c, 8. b

B. 1. my, 2. our, 3. their, 4. their, 5. His, 6. my, 7. his, 8. Their, 9. Her

C. 1. your, 2. I'm, 3. His, 4. Their, 5. She's

1.4

A. 1. number?—7-G, you?—17, address?—17-62 Parsons Avenue 2. live?—Santa Clara, California, from?—Mexico, name?—Clara

B. 1. How old, 2. Where, 3. How old, 4. What, 5. What, 6. Where, 7. Where, 8. What, 9. What, 10. How old

C. 1. How old are you? 2. Where do you live? 3. Where are you from? 4. What is (What's) your name? 5. What is (What's) your phone number?

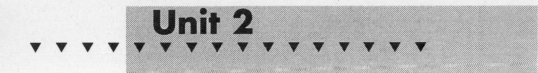

Unit 2

UNIT 2

Unit 2 Grammar Check 2.1 Regular Plurals with -s

A noun is the name of a person, a place, a thing, or an idea.

"Plural" means two or more.

Different nouns have different plural endings.

Add an **s** to most nouns to make them plural.

	plural			plural
name	names		age	ages
date	dates		number	numbers

A. Underline the eight nouns in the list below.
Then look at the picture.
Circle the picture of each noun you underlined.

<u>door</u>	listen	need	light
from	window	paper	middle
book	are	cabinet	spell
chair	pencil	your	what

Name _____   Date _____

B.   Circle the noun. Write the plural in the blank.

1.   what   speak   (book)

     The teacher has three <u>books</u>.

2.   she   pencil   have

     They need two _____.

3.   teacher   put   the

     Listen to the _____.

4.   this   study   chair

     Those are _____.

5.   cabinet   spell   they

     These are _____.

C.   Look at the picture on page 9.
Write the plural forms of all the nouns you circled.

   <u>doors</u>   _____

   _____   _____

   _____   _____

   _____

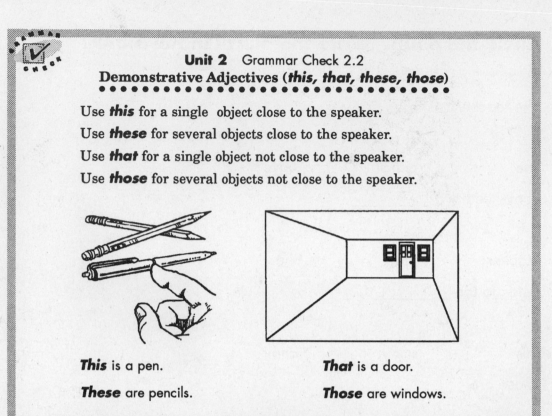

Unit 2 Grammar Check 2.2
Demonstrative Adjectives (*this, that, these, those*)

Use ***this*** for a single object close to the speaker.

Use ***these*** for several objects close to the speaker.

Use ***that*** for a single object not close to the speaker.

Use ***those*** for several objects not close to the speaker.

This is a pen.

These are pencils.

That is a door.

Those are windows.

A.   Circle the correct answer.

1.   (This / These) is my phone number.

2.   (That / Those) are pens.

3.   What are (those / that) in English?

4.   (These / This) are the teacher's books.

5.   (That / Those) is my social security number.

6.   How do you spell (those / that) word?

7.   (This / These) is my son.

8.   (That / Those) is Tina's apartment number.

9.   Take (this / these) book.

10. Close (those / that) windows.

B. **Write** *this, that, these,* **or** *those* **in the blanks. Most sentences have two correct answers.**

1. Excuse me. What are ___*these*___ in English?

2. _____ is your paper.

3. What is _____?

4. _____ is a chair.

5. Give _____ book to John.

6. Turn off _____ light.

7. _____ class is difficult.

8. _____ are the teacher's books.

C. **Read the sentences. Draw things on the desk and on the table.**

This is a book.
This is a notebook.
This is a pen.

That is a calendar.
That is a clock.
That is an eraser.

Unit 2 Grammar Check 2.3
Definite and Indefinite Articles (*a, an, the*)
● ●

Use *a* before consonant sounds b, c, d, f, g, h, j, k, l, m, n, p, q, r, s, t, v, w, x, y, and z.

  a book   *a* class   *a* door

Use *an* when the beginning sound of a word is a vowel sound: a, e, i, o, and u.

  an eraser   *an* office   *an* hour (the *h* isn't pronounced.)

A. Write the first names of classmates in the blanks. Then circle *a* or *an*.

1. There is (ⓐ / an) _Pedro_ in the class.

2. There is (a / an) _____ in the class.

3. There is (a / an) _____ in the class.

4. There is (a / an) _____ in the class.

5. There is (a / an) _____ in the class.

6. There is (a / an) _____ in the class.

7. There is (a / an) _____ in the class.

8. There is (a / an) _____ in the class.

B. Write *a* or *an* in the blanks.

1. _a_ name   6. ____ first name   11. ____ middle name

2. ____ address   7. ____ age   12. ____ phone number

3. ____ last name 8. ____ country   13. ____ date of birth

4. ____ window   9. ____ eraser   14. ____ table

5. ____ clock   10. ____ trash can   15. ____ notebook

Name _____   Date _____

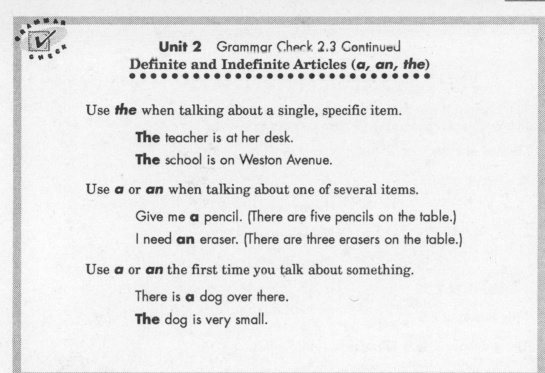

Unit 2   Grammar Check 2.3 Continued
Definite and Indefinite Articles (*a, an, the*)
• •

Use ***the*** when talking about a single, specific item.

The teacher is at her desk.

The school is on Weston Avenue.

Use ***a*** or ***an*** when talking about one of several items.

Give me **a** pencil. (There are five pencils on the table.)

I need **an** eraser. (There are three erasers on the table.)

Use ***a*** or ***an*** the first time you talk about something.

There is **a** dog over there.

The dog is very small.

C.   Write *a, an,* or *the* **in the blanks.**

My name is Ali Aslan. I study English at __a__ school in New York
                                            1

City. _____ city is very big. _____ address of my school is 770 Eighth
         2   3

Avenue.

My class is at 7:00. There is _____ clock outside the school and
                                 4

also _____ clock inside the classroom. _____ clock outside the school is
       5   6

very large. All the students look at it as they go to class.

Today _____ teacher is teaching a grammar lesson. First she
         7

writes ten words on _____ blackboard. Then she says, "Take out _____
                       8   9

piece of paper. Look at _____ blackboard. Write _____ word or two on
                          10   11

your paper. "

Unit 2 Grammar Check 2.4
Present Tense Statements, Regular Verbs
• •

The present tense shows that an action happens again and again. It may happen every day for many weeks or years.

I **leave** at 4:00.

You **leave** at 3:00.

He **leaves** at 12:00.

She **leaves** at 11:00.

It **leaves** at 10:00.

We **leave** at 2:00.

They **leave** at 7:00.

The present tense is also used to state a fact.

Lu **speaks** three languages.

A. Circle the correct word.

1. I ((live) / lives) in Los Angeles.

2. He (speak / speaks) Chinese.

3. It (start / starts) at 2:00.

4. They (give / gives) me money.

5. She (read / reads) very well.

6. You (listen / listens) carefully.

7. We (leave / leaves) school at 4:30.

8. He (draw / draws) pictures.

9. They (stand / stands) at the corner.

10. I (open / opens) the door.

B.   Add an *s* if needed.

1.   He turn __*s*__ on the light.

2.   They turn ___ off the light.

3.   We give ___ them money.

4.   I read ___ a newspaper every day.

5.   You leave ___ at 2:00.

6.   She erase ___ the words.

7.   They put ___ the paper away.

8.   He close ___ the door.

9.   We close ___ the windows.

10. She sit ___ on the desk.

C.   Write a word from the box in each blank. Use each word once. Add an *s* if needed.

leave	teach	ask
put ✓	speak	erase

1.   Please __*put*__ it on the table.

2.   Does Mr. Chapman _____ English?

3.   We _____ Chinese.

4.   She _____ questions in class.

5.   They _____ before 3:00.

6.   The teacher _____ the blackboard.

2.1

A. door, light, window, paper, book, cabinet, chair, pencil

B. 1. books, 2. pencils, 3. teachers, 4. chairs, 5. cabinets

C. doors, lights, windows, papers, books, cabinets, chairs, pencils

2.2

A. 1. This, 2. Those, 3. those, 4. These, 5. That, 6. that, 7. This, 8. That, 9. this, 10. those

B. 1. those (or these), 2. This (or That), 3. this (or that), 4. That (or This), 5. this (or that), 6. this (or that), 7. This (or That), 8.These (or Those)

C. The drawing should show a book, notebook, and a pen on the desk in front of the man, and a calendar, a clock, and an eraser on the table near him.

2.3

A. a Pedro. Use *a* before names beginning with a consonant and *an* before names beginning with a vowel.

B. 1. a, 2. an, 3. a, 4. a, 5. a, 6. a, 7. an, 8. a, 9. an, 10. a, 11. a, 12. a, 13. a, 14. a, 15. a

C. 1. a, 2. The, 3. The, 4. a, 5. a, 6. The, 7. the, 8. the, 9. a, 10. the, 11. a

2.4

A. 1. live, 2. speaks, 3. starts, 4. give, 5. reads, 6. listen, 7. leave, 8. draws, 9. stand, 10. open

B. 1. s, 6. s, 8. s, 10. s

C. 1. put, 2. teach (speak), 3. speak (teach), 4. asks, 5. leave, 6. erases

Unit 3

UNIT 3

Unit 3 Grammar Check 3.1 **Possessives**

Adding an **'s** to a noun shows that the following noun belongs to the **'s** noun.

My mother has a brother.

My mother**'s** brother lives in Miami.

My sister lives in Boston.

My sister**'s** address is 332 Colonial Avenue.

A. Circle the correct word.

1. (Bills / **Bill's**) phone number is 665-8980.

2. What is your (parents / mother's) address?

3. Do you know (Kims / Kim's) apartment number?

4. Do you read (books / book's)?

5. His (sisters / sister's) are teachers.

6. His (sisters / sister's) name is Alma.

B. Add s to plural nouns. Add 's to possessive nouns.

1. My father __'s__ brother is my uncle.

2. I have three uncle___.

3. How many sister___ do you have?

4. Where do your brother___ live?

5. My brother___ name is Lee.

6. My son lives with my parent___.

C. Read each sentence. Then write an 's possessive in each blank.

1. Martha has a pretty baby.

   ___Martha's___ baby is pretty.

2. Ramon has a married son.

   _____ son is married.

3. I have a sister named Maria.

   My _____ name is Maria.

4. My daughter is married. Her husband is tall.

   My _____ husband is tall.

5. My husband has a sister. She is a teacher.

   My _____ sister is a teacher.

6. Ali lives in New York. His phone number is 212-555-5655.

   _____ phone number is 212-555-5655.

7. My father has a small apartment.

   My _____ apartment is small.

8. The teacher has a big desk.

   The _____ desk is big.

Unit 3 Grammar Check 3.2
Comparative Adjectives and Superlative Adjectives
● ●

Adjectives describe people, places, and things.

a *tall* woman   a *little* boy

Use *-er than* to compare two people or things.

Maria is young**er than** Anna.

Pedro is tall**er than** Ivan.

Use *the* + adjective + *-est* to compare more than two people or things.

New York is *the* larg**est** city in the U.S.

I am *the* old**est** child in my family.

A.   Circle the correct word.

1.   Texas is the (larger / (largest)) state in the U.S.
2.   Brazil is (bigger / biggest) than Texas.
3.   What is the (smaller / smallest) state in the U.S.?
4.   Is New York (smaller / smallest) than Florida?
5.   Are you the (older / oldest) child in your family?
6.   Juan is the (shorter / shortest) boy in the class.
7.   Tina is (younger / youngest) than her sister.
8.   My sister is (taller / tallest) than me.

B.   Circle a, b, or c.

1.   My grandfather is   a. old   than my grandmother.
                           (b.) older
                            c. oldest

2.   My father is very   a. tall.
                            b. taller.
                            c. tallest.

3. Nancy is the   a. young   child in the family.
                                b. younger
                                c. youngest

4. There are three pencils on the table. I want the   a. short   one.
                                               b. shorter
                                               c. shortest

5. Chantanavong is a   a. long   name.
                                   b. longer
                                   c. longest

6. The name Chantanavong is   a. long   than the name Smith.
                                           b. longer
                                           c. longest

C.   Look at the chart. Then write sentences using -er.

Name	Age	Height
Larry	45 years old	6 feet tall
Sally	40 years old	5 feet tall
Andy	10 years old	4 feet tall
Tara	3 years old	3 feet tall

1. (Larry / Sally / old)

     Larry is older than Sally.

2. (Tara / Andy / young)

     _____

3. (Larry / Andy / tall)

     _____

4. (Andy / Larry / short)

     _____

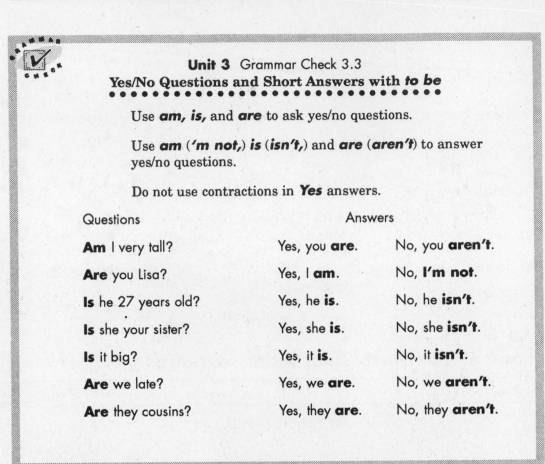

Unit 3 Grammar Check 3.3
Yes/No Questions and Short Answers with *to be*
• •

Use ***am, is,*** and ***are*** to ask yes/no questions.

Use ***am*** (***'m not,***) ***is*** (***isn't,***) and ***are*** (***aren't***) to answer yes/no questions.

Do not use contractions in **Yes** answers.

Questions	Answers	
Am I very tall?	Yes, you **are**.	No, you **aren't**.
Are you Lisa?	Yes, I **am**.	No, **I'm not**.
Is he 27 years old?	Yes, he **is**.	No, he **isn't**.
Is she your sister?	Yes, she **is**.	No, she **isn't**.
Is it big?	Yes, it **is**.	No, it **isn't**.
Are we late?	Yes, we **are**.	No, we **aren't**.
Are they cousins?	Yes, they **are**.	No, they **aren't**.

A.   Match the questions with the answers.

1. Is Maria your aunt?   No, they aren't.
    Am I late?   Yes, you are.
    Are Bill and Jim at school today?   Yes, she is.

2. Are you busy?   No, he isn't.
    Are the children very young?   No, I'm not.
    Is John married?   Yes, they are.

3. Is Larry a father?   Yes, I am.
    Is Aunt Amy 27 years old?   No, she isn't.
    Are you happy?   Yes, he is.

B. Look at the box on page 21. Then complete the short answers below.

1. Are you married?   Yes, ____I am____.
2. Is Peter tall?   No, _____.
3. Is Laura 40 years old?   Yes, _____.
4. Are we in French class?   No, _____.
5. Am I funny?   Yes, _____.
6. Are you tired?   No, _____.
7. Is Mr. Ono at home?   Yes, _____.
8. Am I serious?   No, _____.
9. Are Andy and Carol teachers? Yes, _____.
10. Is Susan very young?   No, _____.

C. Look at the box on page 21. Write the question and the answer.

1. (Mrs. Ames / friendly)   ___Is Mrs. Ames friendly___?
    (Yes)   ___Yes, she is___.

2. (Bill and Ted / tall)   _____?
    (No)   _____.

3. (We / late)   _____?
    (Yes)   _____.

4. (I / thin)   _____?
    (No)   _____.

5. (You / my cousin)   _____?
    (Yes)   _____.

Unit 3 Grammar Check 3.4
Present Tense Statements with *to have*
● ●

Have is not a regular verb. It has two forms: **have** and **has**.

| I | **have** | short hair. |
| You | **have** | dark eyes. |

He	**has**	blue eyes.
She	**has**	long hair.
It	**has**	big eyes.

| We | **have** | curly hair. |
| They | **have** | straight hair. |

A. Circle the correct word.

1. I (have / has) brown eyes.

2. They (have / has) a big apartment.

3. Carol (have / has) light skin.

4. You and I (have / has) dark skin.

5. You (have / has) a class now.

6. Jim (have / has) two brothers.

7. Jim's brothers (have / has) curly hair.

8. Carol and Jim (have / has) a serious teacher.

9. We (have / has) a small classroom.

10. Ms. Albert (have / has) no children.

B. Write the word *have* or *has* in each blank.

The Santos family lives in Denver, Colorado. They __have__ a
                                                      1
big house. It _____ nine rooms. Billy Santos _____ a small
              2   3
bedroom on the second floor. It _____ two windows. Mr. and Mrs.
                                4
Santos _____ the biggest bedroom. It _____ five windows.
       5   6
   Mr. and Mrs. Santos _____ three children. Manuel is the
                       7
oldest. He _____ short, curly hair. He is in high school and
           8
_____ a job after school every day.
9
   The two younger children are girls. Iris is ten and Lucia is twelve.

They both _____ big dark eyes. Iris _____ long hair
          10   11
and Lucia _____ short hair. They _____ a pet cat. It
          12   13
_____ green eyes. The cat _____ its own bed in the
14   15
girls' room. Mrs. Santos says the cat is like her fourth child.

C. Write the word *am, is, are, have,* or *has* in the blank.
1. What __is__ your first name?
2. Alice _____ two middle names.
3. She _____ a friendly face.
4. She _____ 18 years old.
5. Alice's sister and brother _____ in high school.
6. They _____ two classes together.
7. Alice's father _____ two jobs.
8. He _____ a teacher during the day. At night he works in a store.
9. Alice's family _____ very friendly.
10. I _____ happy to know them.

3.1

A. 1. Bill's, 2. mother's, 3. Kim's, 4. books, 5. sisters, 6. sister's

B. 1. 's, 2. s, 3. s, 4. s, 5. 's, 6. s

C. 1. Martha's, 2. Ramon's, 3. sister's, 4. daughter's, 5. husband's, 6. Ali's, 7. father's, 8. teacher's

3.2

A. 1. largest, 2. bigger, 3. smallest, 4. smaller, 5. oldest, 6. shortest, 7. younger, 8. taller

B. 1. b, 2. a, 3. c, 4. c, 5. a, 6. b

C. 1. Larry is older than Sally. 2. Tara is younger than Andy. 3. Larry is taller than Andy. 4. Andy is shorter than Larry

3.3

A. 1. aunt?—Yes, she is. late?—Yes, you are. today?—No, they aren't, 2. busy?—No, I'm not.young?—Yes, they are. married?—No, he isn't. 3. father?—Yes, he is. old?—No, she isn't.happy?—Yes, I am.

B. 1. I am, 2. he isn't, 3. she is, 4. we aren't, 5. you are, 6. I'm not, 7. he is, 8. you aren't, 9. they are, 10. she isn't

C. 1. Is Mrs. Ames friendly? Yes, she is. 2. Are Bill and Ted tall? No, they aren't. 3. Are we late? Yes, we are. 4. Am I thin? No, you aren't. 5. Are you my cousin? Yes, I am.

3.4

A. 1. have, 2. have, 3. has, 4. have, 5. have, 6. has, 7. have, 8. have, 9. have, 10. has

B. 1. have, 2. has, 3. has, 4. has, 5. have, 6. has, 7. have, 8. has, 9. has, 10. have, 11. has, 12. has, 13. have, 14. has, 15. has

C. 1. is, 2. has, 3. has, 4. is, 5. are, 6. have, 7. has, 8. is, 9. is, 10. am

Unit 4

UNIT
4

Unit 4 Grammar Check 4.1 **Regular Plurals with -es**

You add an **-s** to most nouns to make them plural.

| door | door**s** | page | page**s** |
| room | room**s** | closet | closet**s** |

You add an **-es** to nouns ending in ss, ch, sh, and x to make them plural. (Pronunciation help: the plural form has two syllables.)

| class | class**es** | dish | dish**es** |
| porch | porch**es** | box | box**es** |

A. Write *s* or *es* in the first blank. Write the plural in the second blank.

1. class   + _es_   = _classes_
2. yard   + _s_   = _yards_
3. porch   + _____ = _____
4. hall   + _____ = _____
5. dish   + _____ = _____
6. box   + _____ = _____
7. kitchen   + _____ = _____
8. aunt   + _____ = _____
9. church   + _____ = _____
10. wish   + _____ = _____

B. Circle the correct spellings.

1. There are two (bushs / (bushes)) in front of the house.
2. There are three (rooms / roomes) in my apartment.
3. Those (windows / windowes) are very big.
4. I got two (watchs / watches) for my birthday.
5. We ate some (sandwichs / sandwiches) for lunch.

C. Look at the pictures. Write the plural form of each word.

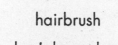

hairbrush

1. <u>hairbrushes</u>

box

2. _____

bookcase

3. _____

dress

4. _____

sofa

5. _____

stove

6. _____

bench

7. _____

lamp

8. _____

sandwich

9. _____

Unit 4   Grammar Check 4.2
Questions with *Is there...?* and *Are there...?*
• •

Is there and ***Are there*** are used to ask questions about objects and their locations.

The answers to these questions are: ***Yes, there is.***

No, there isn't.

Yes, there are.

No, there aren't.

Is there a bed in the bedroom?

    Yes, there is.   ***No, there isn't.***

Are there towels in the bathroom?

    Yes, there are.   ***No, there aren't.***

A.   **Write** *Is there* **or** *Are there* **in each blank.**

1.   <u>Are there</u>   pots and pans in the kitchen?

2.   _____   books in the library?

3.   _____   a dresser in the bedroom?

4.   _____   towels in the bathroom?

5.   _____   a book on your desk?

6.   _____   dishes in the sink?

7.   _____   pillows on the bed?

8.   _____   curtains on the window?

9.   _____   a chair by the table?

10.   _____   a bookcase in your classroom?

Name _____ Date _____

B. **Look at the picture. Write questions and answers about it using** *there is* **and** *there are.*

1. (chair / living room)   <u>Is there a chair in the living room</u>   ?
    <u>Yes, there is</u>   .

2. (chair / bedroom)   _____   ?
    _____ .

3. (towels / living room)   _____   ?
    _____ .

4. (bed / living room)   _____   ?
    _____ .

5. (rug / bedroom)   _____   ?
    _____ .

6. (curtains / living room)   _____   ?
    _____ .

7. (tables / bedroom)   _____   ?
    _____ .

8. (sofa / living room)   _____   ?
    _____ .

Unit 4 Grammar Check 4.3
Present Tense Questions and Short Answers
• •
Use **do** and **does** to ask present tense questions.

The short answers also use **do, does, don't,** and **doesn't**.

Do I have white hair?	Yes, you **do**.	No, you **don't**.
Do you live alone?	Yes, I **do**.	No, I **don't**.
Does he have a car?	Yes, he **does**.	No, he **doesn't**.
Does she have a house?	Yes, she **does**.	No, she **doesn't**.
Does it have a yard?	Yes, it **does**.	No, it **doesn't**.
Do we need help?	Yes, we **do**.	No, we **don't**.
Do they drink coffee?	Yes, they **do**.	No, they **don't**.

A.   Circle the correct word.

1. (Do / **Does**) he wash the dishes?   Yes, he (do / **does**).

2. (Do / Does) you clean the house?   No, I (don't / doesn't).

3. (Do / Does) they make their beds?   No, they (don't / doesn't).

4. (Do / Does) she sleep eight hours?   Yes, she (do / does).

5. (Do / Does) I talk too much?   No, you (don't / doesn't).

6. (Do / Does) you cook dinner?   No, I (don't / doesn't).

7. (Do / Does) he eat breakfast?   Yes, he (do / does).

8. (Do / Does) they iron their clothes?   Yes, they (do / does).

9. (Do / Does) she have children?   No, she (don't / doesn't).

10. (Do / Does) it end at 4:00?   Yes, it (do / does).

B. **Write** *Do* **or** *Does* **in the blank in each question.**
   Write *do, don't, does* **or** *doesn't* **in the blank in**
   each answer.

1. ___*Do*___ you wash your face every night?
    Yes, I ___*do*___.

2. _____ Mr. Lewis live in Detroit?
    No, he _____.

3. _____ your family eat dinner together?
    Yes, we _____.

4. _____ Maria read the newspaper every day?
    Yes, she _____.

5. _____ I get up early?
    No, you _____.

6. _____ your children set the table?
    No, they _____.

C. **Write the questions and answers. Give real answers.**

1. (you / eat breakfast every day) _Do you eat breakfast every day_ ?
    _Yes, I do_____.

2. (your teacher / have black hair) _____?
    _____.

3. (your classroom / have a window)_____?
    _____.

4. (you / iron clothes) _____?
    _____.

5. (your mother / live with you) _____?
    _____.

Unit 4 Grammar Check 4.4 **Present Continuous Statements**

The present continuous tense shows that an action is happening now.

Present continuous verbs have two parts:

1. **am, is,** or **are**

2. a verb + **–ing**

I **am doing** the laundry.

You **are ironing** clothes.

He **is listening** to music.

She **is reading** the newspaper.

It **is sleeping**.

We **are watching** TV.

They **are cleaning** the house.

A. Write the word *am, is,* or *are* **in the blank.**

1. We ___are___ studying English.

2. Carlos _____ reading a book.

3. Mr. and Mrs. Koch _____ taking care of the children.

4. I _____ cleaning the house.

5. Louisa _____ talking on the phone.

6. You _____ wearing my shirt.

7. He _____ sleeping right now.

8. You and I _____ working hard.

9. The children _____ getting dressed.

10. The teacher _____ looking at the clock.

Name _____ Date _____

B. Write a present continuous statement under each picture.

1. <u>She's making the bed.</u>

2. _____

3. _____

4. _____

5. _____

6. _____

7. _____

8. _____

Unit 4   Grammar Check 4.5
Present Tense Questions with *What time...?*
• •

What time...? questions use the words **do** and **does**.

The answer to a ***what time...?*** question often starts with **at** + a clock time.

What time **do** I leave for work?	At 8:00.
What time **do** you get home?	At 5:00.
What time **does** she get up?	At 7:00.
What time **does** he have breakfast?	At 8:00.
What time **does** it start?	At 9:00.
What time **do** we leave?	At 7:30.
What time **do** they get on the bus?	At 5:30.

A.   Circle the correct word.

1.   What time (**do** / does) they go to bed?

2.   What time (do / does) she feed the children?

3.   What time (do / does) he get to work?

4.   What time (do / does) Mr. and Mrs. Chin get home?

5.   What time (do / does) I get on the bus?

6.   What time (do / does) you go to bed on Fridays?

7.   What time (do / does) they leave class?

8.   What time (do / does) Mona call home?

9.   What time (do / does) we have lunch?

10. What time (do / does) the children get up on Saturdays?

B. **Write a question and answer under each picture. The sentences on page 33 will help you find the words you need.**

1. <u>What time does he get up?</u>

2. <u>He gets up at 7:00.</u>

5. _____

6. _____

9. _____

10. _____

3. _____

4. _____

7. _____

8. _____

11. _____

12. _____

4.1

A. 1. es=classes, 2. s=yards, 3. es=porches, 4. s=halls, 5. es=dishes, 6. es=boxes, 7. s=kitchens, 8. s=aunts, 9. es=churches, 10. es=wishes

B. 1. bushes, 2. rooms, 3. windows, 4. watches, 5. sandwiches

C. 1. hairbrushes, 2. boxes, 3. bookcases, 4. dresses, 5. sofas, 6. stoves, 7. benches, 8. lamps, 9. sandwiches

4.2

A. 1. Are there, 2. Are there, 3. Is there, 4. Are there, 5. Is there, 6. Are there, 7. Are there, 8. Are there, 9. Is there, 10. Is there

B. 1. Is there a chair in the living room? Yes, there is. 2. Is there a chair in the bedroom? Yes, there is. 3. Are there towels in the living room? No, there aren't. 4. Is there a bed in the living room? No, there isn't. 5. Is there a rug in the bedroom? Yes, there is. 6. Are there curtains in the living room? Yes, there are. 7. Are there tables in the bedroom? No, there aren't. 8. Is there a sofa in the living room? Yes, there is.

4.3

A. 1. Does/does, 2. Do/don't, 3. Do/don't, 4. Does/does, 5. Do/don't, 6. Do/don't, 7. Does/does, 8. Do/do, 9. Does/doesn't, 10. Does/does

B. 1. Do/do, 2. Does/doesn't, 3. Does/do, 4. Does/does, 5. Do/don't, 6. Do/don't

C. 1. Do you eat breakfast every day? Yes, I do. (No, I don't.) 2. Does your teacher have black hair? Yes he/she does. (No, he/she doesn't.) 3. Does your classroom have a window? Yes, it does. (No, it doesn't.) 4. Do you iron clothes? Yes, I do. (No, I don't.) 5. Does your mother live with you? Yes, she does. (No, she doesn't.)

4.4

A. 1. are, 2. is, 3. are, 4. am, 5. is, 6. are, 7. is, 8. are, 9. are, 10. is

B. 1. She's making the bed. 2. He's cleaning (the house). 3. She's cooking, 4. They're reading (the newspaper). 5. He's doing the laundry. 6. He's setting the table. 7. They're eating (dinner). 8. She's washing her face.

4.5

A. 1. do, 2. does, 3. does, 4. do, 5. do, 6. do, 7. do, 8. does, 9. do, 10. do

B. 1. What time does he get up? 2. He gets up at 7:00. 3. What time do they have (eat) breakfast? 4. They have (eat) breakfast at 7:30. 5. What time does she leave for work? 6. She leaves for work at 8:30. 7. What time do they get on the bus? 8. They get on the bus at 3:00. 9. What time does she have (eat) lunch? 10. She has (eats) lunch at noon. 11. What time does he get home? 12. He gets home at 6:00.

Unit 5

5.1   Prepositions of Location

5.2   Prepositions of Time

5.3   Present Tense Questions with
       Where...?

UNIT 5

Unit 5   Grammar Check 5.1   **Prepositions of Location**

When someone asks how to find a building, you use sentences containing prepositions of location to give directions.
You also use prepositions of location to describe locations on a map.

The library is **next to** the school.

The hospital is **in back of** the school.

The library is **between** the restaurant and the school.

The department store is **on the corner of** Third Street.

The movie theater is **in front of** the post office.

The laundromat is **across from** the restaurant.

The laundromat is **near** the movie theater.

The movie theater is **a block from** the restaurant.

The post office is **around the corner from** the movie theater.

The museum is **far from** the department store.

A.   Read the sentences above. Write the name of each building on the picture.

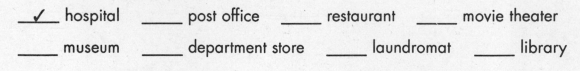

__✓__ hospital   _____ post office   _____ restaurant   _____ movie theater

_____ museum   _____ department store   _____ laundromat   _____ library

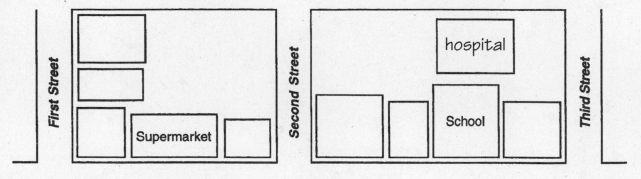

B. **Look at the picture. Answer the questions. There may be more than one correct answer.**

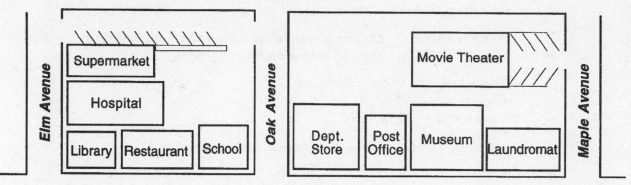

1. Where is the laundromat?

    <u>It's on the corner of Maple Avenue</u>_____.

2. Where is the department store?

    _____.

3. Where is the hospital?

    _____.

4. Where is the school?

    _____.

5. Where is the restaurant?

    _____.

6. Where is the movie theater?

    _____.

7. Where is the post office?

    _____.

8. Where is the library?

    _____.

Unit 5 Grammar Check 5.2 **Prepositions of Time**

The prepositions of time *in, at,* and **on** each have a different use.

In comes before: the words *morning, afternoon,* and *evening*
the names of *months* and *years*

I have breakfast *in* the morning.
Summer starts *in* June.
I came to the U.S. *in* 1995.

At comes before: *clock time, noon,* and *midnight*
the word *night*

Class starts *at* 8:00. We don't have class *at* night.

On comes before: the days of the week

I work *on* Monday. I have class *on* Thursday.

A. Circle *a, b,* **or** *c.*

1. The bank opens   a. in   9:00   (a.) in   the morning.
    b. on   b. on
    (c.) at   c. at

2. My birthday is   a. in   September.
           b. on
           c. at

3. We have dinner   a. in   6:00   a. in   the evening.
    b. on   b. on
    c. at   c. at

4. We have lunch   a. in   noon   a. in   Sundays.
    b. on   b. on
    c. at   c. at

5. I like to sleep for an hour   a. in   the afternoon.
           b. on
           c. at

B. **Make sentences using words from the three columns. You can use a word more than once. There are many possible sentences.**

A	B	C
I am in bed	in	June
We have breakfast	on	Monday
I have class	at	the morning
My birthday is		midnight

1. <u>I am in bed at midnight</u> _____.

2. _____.

3. _____.

4. _____.

C. **Look at the TV schedule. Write** *in, on,* **and** *at* **in the blanks.**

MONDAY		TUESDAY	
10:00	Talk Time	10:00	Talk Time
11:00	Ms. Fix-it	11:00	Cook It
Noon	News		Yourself
1:00	Sail Away	Noon	News
2:00	The Computer	1:00	Sew Right
	Hour	2:00	Kids at play
300	Life is Hard	300	Life is Hard

2. You can see *Sail Away* ___<u>at</u>___ 1:00 ___<u>on</u>___ Monday.

2. You can see *Talk Time* _____ the morning.

3. You can see the news _____ noon.

4. You can see *Life Is Hard* _____ the afternoon.

5. You can see *Sew Right* _____ 1:00 _____ Tuesday.

6. You can see *Kids at play* _____ Tuesday _____ 2:00.

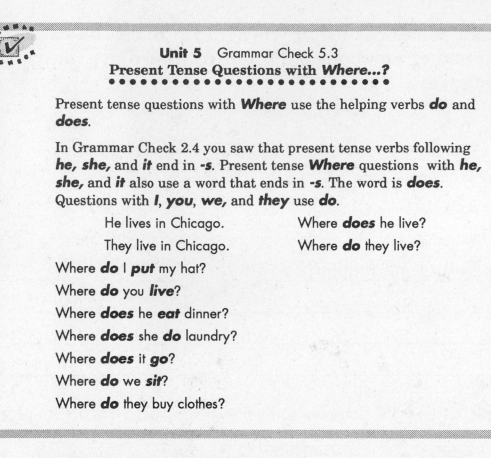

Unit 5   Grammar Check 5.3
Present Tense Questions with *Where...?*
• •

Present tense questions with ***Where*** use the helping verbs ***do*** and ***does***.

In Grammar Check 2.4 you saw that present tense verbs following *he, she,* and *it* end in *-s*. Present tense ***Where*** questions with *he, she,* and *it* also use a word that ends in *-s*. The word is ***does***. Questions with *I, you, we,* and ***they*** use ***do***.

He lives in Chicago.	Where ***does*** he live?
They live in Chicago.	Where ***do*** they live?

Where ***do*** I ***put*** my hat?

Where ***do*** you ***live***?

Where ***does*** he ***eat*** dinner?

Where ***does*** she ***do*** laundry?

Where ***does*** it ***go***?

Where ***do*** we ***sit***?

Where ***do*** they buy clothes?

A.   Circle the correct word.

1.   Where (do / (does)) she buy food?   At the grocery store.

2.   Where (do / does) they live?   In Alabama.

3.   Where (do / does) I sit?   Over there.

4.   Where (do / does) Carol work?   At a bank.

5.   Where (do / does) Jim get money?   At a bank.

6.   Where (do / does) you buy gas?   At a gas station.

7.   Where (do / does) I buy stamps?   At a post office.

8.   Where (do / does) Lee and Debbie live?   In Texas.

9.   Where (do / does) we go after lunch?   To class.

10. Where (do / does) you see movies?   At a movie theater.

B. **Write** *do* **or** *does* **in the blanks.**

1. Where ___*do*___ you find a lot of books?   In the library.

2. Where _____ Edna eat breakfast?   At home.

3. Where _____ Mr. and Mrs. Dean live?   In Idaho.

4. Where _____ Carlos go after school?   Home.

5. Where _____ sick people go?   To the hospital.

C. **Write** *where* **questions that go with each answer. There is more than one correct question for each answer.**

1. (work) _____ Where does Rita work _____?

   At a supermarket.

2. (do laundry) _____?

   At my friend's house.

3. (sleep) _____?

   In the baby's room.

4. (live) _____?

   In a good neighborhood.

5. (get a haircut) _____?

   At a barbershop.

6. (borrow books) _____?

   At a library.

5.1

A. Counter-clockwise from left to right: museum, post office, movie theater, supermarket, laundromat, restaurant, library, school, department store, hospital (behind school)

B. 1. It's on the corner of Maple Avenue. 2. It's next to the post office. (It's on the corner of Oak Avenue.) 3. It's between the library and the supermarket. 4. It's next to the restaurant. (It's on the corner of Oak Avenue.) 5. It's between the library and the school. 6. It's behind the museum. 7. It's between the department store and the museum. 8. It's on the corner of Elm Avenue. It's in front of the hospital. (Other answers are possible.)

5.2

A. 1. c/a, 2. a, 3. c/a, 4. c/b, 5. a

B. I am in bed at midnight. We have breakfast in the morning. I have class in the morning. My birthday is in June. (Other answers are possible.)

C. 1. at/on, 2. in, 3. at, 4. in, 5. at/on, 6. on/at

5.3

A. 1. does, 2. do, 3. do, 4. does, 5. does, 6. do, 7. do, 8. do, 9. do, 10. do

B. 1. do, 2. does, 3. do, 4. does, 5. do

C. 1. Where does Rita work? 2. Where do you do your laundry? 3. Where do you sleep? 4. Where do they live? 5. Where do you get a haircut? 6. Where does she borrow books? (Other answers are possible.)

Unit 6

UNIT
6

Unit 6 Grammar Check 6.1
Want to + a Verb, Questions and Statements
• •

The phrase **want to** / **wants to** is followed by the simple form of the verb in both questions and answers.

I want to **be** a teacher.   He wants to **leave** a message.

Do you want to **see** a movie?   Does he want to **have** lunch?

In Grammar Check 5.3 you saw that present tense short answers use **do** and **does**. Present tense short answers with **want to** also use **do** and **does**.

Do you want to go now?   Yes, I **do.**   No, I **don't.**

Does she want to buy it?   Yes, she **does.**   No, she **doesn't.**

A. Circle the correct word and complete the short answers.

1. (Do / Does) you want to work as a manager?   Yes, I _do_ .

2. Antonia (want / wants) to live in El Paso.

3. She wants to (eat / eats) dinner at home.

4. Angel wants to (buy / buys) a car.

5. (Do / Does) Ester want to have children?   No, _____.

6. We want (watch / to watch) TV now.

7. They (want / wants) to go to the bank.

8. Hector wants to (listen / listens) to music.

9. I (want / wants) to get a job.

10. (Do / Does) Mr. and Mrs. Leon want to leave?   Yes, _____.

B. **Make statements or questions using words from the three columns. You can use a word more than once.**

A	B	C
Do	want to	go home.
Does	wants to	be a bank teller.
I	they	wants to study Spanish.
Ben and Jean	the children	want to leave now?
Gloria	she	visit Miami.
Alan	you	wants to go to sleep.

1. Do they want to leave now?

2. _____

3. _____

4. _____

5. _____

C. **Rewrite each statement as a question.**

1. Tien wants to eat dinner.

    Does Tien want to eat dinner _____ ?

2. They want to listen to music.

    _____ ?

3. Ali wants to go to college someday.

    _____ ?

4. Mr. Wang wants to buy a new computer.

    _____ ?

Unit 6   Grammar Check 6.2
Present Perfect Tense Questions and Answers
· ·

The present perfect tense shows how long something has been happening. It uses two different verbs:
the verb **to have** + the past participle form of another verb.

	VERB **to have**	PAST PARTICIPLE OF ANOTHER VERB	
	⇩	⇩	
How long	**have** you	**worked**	there?
I	**have**	**worked**	there for six months.
How long	**has** she	**lived**	here?
She	**has**	**lived**	here for two years.

(If you wish, review Grammar Check 3.4, **have** and **has**.)

A.   Write a past participle from the box in each blank.

Simple Form	Past Participle	Simple Form	Past Participle
work	worked	know	known
live	lived	study	studied
listen	listened	be	been
watch	watched		

1.   How long have they ___lived___ in that apartment?

   They have ___lived___ there for two years.

2.   How long has she _____ Jose?

   She has _____ him for four years.

3.   How long has she _____ at the factory?

   She has _____ there for six months.

4.   How long have you _____ English?

   I have _____ English for two years.

B. **Write *how long* questions using the present perfect tense. Use the words to make questions. Check the box on page 43.**

1. (he / live in Dallas)

    <u>How long has he lived in Dallas</u> _____ ?

2. (They / know Mr. Jenkins)

    _____ ?

3. (I / work as a cashier)

    _____ ?

4. (you / study Spanish)

    _____ ?

5. (Min / be a bank teller)

    _____ ?

C. **Write four new sentences from exercise B. as present perfect statements. Use the time expressions. (Check the box on page 43.)**

1. (six years)

    <u>He has lived in Dallas for six years</u> _____ .

2. (two months)

    _____ .

3. (ten years)

    _____ .

4. (six months)

    _____ .

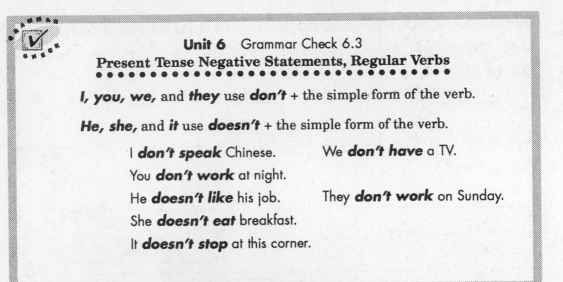

Unit 6 Grammar Check 6.3
Present Tense Negative Statements, Regular Verbs
• •

I, you, we, and ***they*** use ***don't*** + the simple form of the verb.

He, she, and *it* use ***doesn't*** + the simple form of the verb.

I ***don't speak*** Chinese.   We ***don't have*** a TV.
You ***don't work*** at night.
He ***doesn't like*** his job.   They ***don't work*** on Sunday.
She ***doesn't eat*** breakfast.
It ***doesn't stop*** at this corner.

A.   Circle the correct word.

1. I (don't / doesn't) like milk.

2. He (don't / doesn't) speak Chinese.

3. It (don't / doesn't) start at 3:00.

4. They (don't / doesn't) have a car.

5. She (don't / doesn't) study in the library.

6. You (don't / doesn't) know my sister.

7. We (don't / doesn't) eat lunch at home.

8. He (don't / doesn't) put his money in the bank.

9. They (don't / doesn't) live with their parents.

10. I (don't / doesn't) watch TV.

B. Write *don't* **or** *doesn't* **in the blanks.**

1. He _*doesn't*_ live near me.

2. They _____ work as secretaries.

3. We _____ do the laundry at night.

4. I _____ get up at 6:00 every day.

5. You _____ leave the house by 9:00.

6. She _____ read a newspaper every day.

7. They _____ turn off all the lights at night.

8. He _____ want to go home now.

9. We _____ close the windows at night.

10. She _____ teach French on Saturdays.

C. Change each sentence into a negative statement.

1. She sleeps all day long.

    _She doesn't sleep all day long_____.

2. Judy and Claire have two cats.

    _____.

3. I get here at 9:00 every day.

    _____.

4. Jim does his homework at night.

    _____.

5. You set the table before dinner.

    _____.

6. Class starts at 9:30.

    _____.

Unit 6 Grammar Check 6.4
Yes/No Questions and Short Answers with Present Tense

I, you, we, and *they* use *do* + the simple form of the verb for questions.

I, you, we, and *they* use *do* or *don't* for short answers.

He, she and *it* use *does* + the simple form of the verb for questions.

I, you, we, and *they* use *does* or *doesn't* for short answers.

Do I *know* you?	Yes, you *do.*	No, you *don't.*
Do you *have* a computer?	Yes, I *do.*	No, I *don't.*
Does he *like* his job?	Yes, he *does.*	No, he *doesn't.*
Does she *study* hard?	Yes, she *does.*	No, she *doesn't.*
Does it *work*?	Yes, it *does.*	No, it *doesn't.*
Do we eat too much?	Yes, we *do.*	No, we *don't.*
Do they *sell* TVs?	Yes, they *do.*	No, they *don't.*

A. Circle the correct word.

1. (Do / (Does)) she live with her brother?

   No, she (don't / (doesn't)).

2. (Do / Does) your family watch a lot of TV?

   Yes, they (do / does).

3. (Do / Does) Richard work hard?

   Yes, he (do / does).

4. (Do / Does) you and I like the same music?

   No, we (don't / doesn't).

B.   **Write** *do, does, don't* **or** *doesn't* **in the blanks.**

1.   ___Do___ the students like this class?

  Yes, they ___do___.

2.   _____ you get up early?

  No, I _____.

3.   _____ Mr. Ricardi have long hair?

  Yes, he _____.

4.   _____ Ellie make clothes for her children?

  No, she _____.

5.   _____ we talk too much?

  Yes, we _____.

6.   _____ Carlos study a lot?

  No, he _____.

C.   **Write yes/no questions. Use the words to make questions. Then answer each question.**

1.   (Betty   have an apartment   yes)

  Does Betty have an apartment _____?

  Yes, she does _____.

2.   (the Greens   own a computer   no)

  _____?

  _____.

3.   (you   take care of sick people   no)

  _____?

  _____.

4.   (Pedro   throw out the garbage   no)

  _____?

  _____.

Unit 6 Grammar Check 6.5
Present Continuous Versus Simple Present
• •

In Grammar Check 2.4 (Present Tense Statements) you saw that the present tense describes everyday actions.

You also saw that **he, she,** and **it** forms end in **-s**.

In Grammar Check 4.4 (Present Continuous Statements) you saw that the present continuous tense shows that an action is happening now.

You also saw that it has two parts:

- **am, is,** or **are**

- a verb + **-ing** ending

In this lesson you will practice using both tenses together.

A.   Circle the correct answer.

1.   Maria (speaks / is speaking) English at work every day.

2.   Please be quiet! The baby (sleeps / is sleeping).

3.   Look at Ivan. He (wears / is wearing) Sally's hat.

4.   Chan always (speaks / is speaking) Chinese with his mother.

5.   The baby (drinks / is drinking) three bottles of milk every day.

6.   I can't go with you right now. I (watch / am watching) television.

7.   They (study / are studying) English every night.

8.   It's cold today so she (wears / is wearing) a sweater.

B. **Look at the pictures. Then look at the words after each number. Use these words to write statements in the present tense and the present continuous tense.**

Now. ➡

At the office every day. ➡

1. (he / wear / jeans)
   He is wearing jeans now _____.

   (he / wear / a suit)
   He wears a suit at the office _____.

2. (he / drink / coffee)
   _____.

   (he / drink / soda)
   _____.

3. (he / read / the newspaper)
   _____.

   (he / read / a book)
   _____.

Answer Key

▼ ▼ ▼ ▼ ▼ ▼ ▼ ▼ ▼ ▼ ▼ ▼ ▼ ▼ ▼ ▼

6.1

A. 1. Do/I do, 2. wants, 3. eat, 4. buy, 5. Does/she doesn't, 6. to watch, 7. want, 8. listen, 9. want, 10. Do/they do

B. 1. Do they want to leave now? 2. Does she want to leave now? 3. I want to visit Miami. 4. Ben and Jean want to go home. 5. Gloria wants to go home. 6. Alan wants to visit Miami. (Other answers are possible.)

C. 1. Does Tien want to eat dinner? 2. Do they want to listen to music? 3. Does Ali want to go to college someday? 4. Does Mr. Wang want to buy a new computer?

6.2

A. 1. lived/lived, 2. known/known, 3. worked/worked, 4. studied/studied

B. 1. How long has he lived in Dallas? 2. How long have they known Mr. Jenkins? 3. How long have I worked as a cashier? 4. How long have you studied Spanish? 5. How long has Min been a bank teller?

C. 1. He has lived in Dallas for six years. 2. They have known Mr. Jenkins for two months. 3. I have worked as a cashier for ten years. 4. You have studied Spanish for six months.(Other answers are possible.)

6.3

A. 1. don't, 2. doesn't, 3. doesn't, 4. don't, 5. doesn't, 6. don't, 7. don't, 8. doesn't, 9. don't, 10. don't

B. 1. doesn't, 2. don't, 3. don't, 4. don't, 5. don't, 6. doesn't, 7. don't, 8. doesn't, 9. don't, 10. doesn't

C. 1. She doesn't sleep all day long. 2. Judy and Claire don't have two cats. 3. I don't get here at 9:00 every day. 4. Jim doesn't do his homework at night. 5. You don't set the table before dinner. 6. Class doesn't start at 9:30.

6.4

A. 1. Does/doesn't, 2. Does/do, 3. Does/does, 4. Do/don't

B. 1. Do/do, 2. Do/don't, 3. Does/does, 4. Does/doesn't, 5. Do/do, 6. Does/doesn't

C. 1. Does Betty have an apartment? Yes, she does. 2. Do the Greens own a computer? No, they don't. 3. Do you take care of sick people? No, I don't. 4. Does Pedro throw out the garbage? No, he doesn't.

6.5

A. 1. speaks, 2. is sleeping, 3. is wearing, 4. speaks, 5. drinks, 6. am watching, 7. study, 8. is wearing

B. 1. He is wearing jeans now. He wears a suit at the office. 2. He drinks coffee at the office. He is drinking soda now. 3. He reads the newspaper at the office. He is reading a book now.

Unit 7

UNIT 7

Unit 7 Grammar Check 7.1 **Plurals with -ies**

In Grammar Check 2.1 you saw that most plural nouns end in **-s**.

| name | name**s** | age | age**s** |

In this lesson you will see plural nouns with **-ies** endings.

| country | countr**ies** | nationality | nationalit**ies** |
| dictionary | dictionar**ies** | family | famil**ies** |

These nouns end in a consonant plus a **-y**.

(The consonants are b, c, d, f, g, h, j, k, l, m, n, p, q, r, s, t, v, w, x, and z. The other letters, a, e, i, o, u, and sometimes y, are called vowels.)

To make these nouns plural, do two things:

    1) change the **-y** to **-i**

    2) add **-es**.

countr**y** ⇨ countr**i** ⇨ + **es** = countr**ies**

> Nouns that end in a vowel plus a **-y**, have regular plurals
>
> | day | day**s** | chimney | chimney**s** |

A. Write the plural of each noun.

1. library   <u>libraries</u>   5. pharmacy   _____

2. face   _____   6. baby   _____

3. city   _____   7. box   _____

4. party   _____   8. secretary   _____

B.   Circle the noun. Write the plural in the blank.

1.   lay   pretty   (lady)

There are three __ladies__ in the office.

2.   buy   pharmacy   busy

There are two _____ on Main Street.

3.   secretary   friendly   heavy

The boss has two _____ .

4.   pretty   city   the

New York and Chicago are big _____ .

5.   french fry   very   day

These _____ are delicious!

C.   Write the plurals of these words. Review Grammar Check 2.1 (Regular Plurals) and Grammar Check 4.1 (Plurals with -es).

1.	box	__boxes__	10. fruit	_____
2.	kiss	_____	11. story	_____
3.	turkey	_____	12. dash	_____
4.	fly	_____	13. city	_____
5.	class	_____	14. pencil	_____
6.	library	_____	15. sandwich	_____
7.	boy	_____	16. party	_____
8.	baby	_____	17. chimney	_____
9.	glass	_____	18. church	_____

Unit 7   Grammar Check 7.2   **Adverbs of Frequency**

Adverbs of frequency show how often something happens. They usually come before the verb in the sentence.

always 100%	usually 80%	sometimes 50%	rarely 10%	never 0%
all the time	almost all the time	not all the time	almost never	at no time
every day	almost every day	some days	one day a year	

I **rarely** eat meat.   (once or twice a year)

I **sometimes** eat fish.   (once a month)

Adverbs of frequency come before the verb.

I **usually** have breakfast at home.

I **always** drive to work.

A.   Circle the adverbs of frequency in these sentences.

1.   I (always) bring lunch to work.

2.   The teacher sometimes takes the students to the museum.

3.   My sister rarely does the laundry.

4.   I never miss class.

5.   We usually have class on Friday morning.

6.   I usually wait at the bus stop.

7.   They never shop at the supermarket.

8.   Antonio always hangs his coat in the closet.

B. Look at the chart. Then write sentences using adverbs of frequency.

	always	usually	sometimes	rarely	never
eggs		Alma			Oscar
orange juice	I		Delia		
cereal				Chantavong	
muffins		Howard			

1. (Delia   drink orange juice)

    <u>Delia sometimes drinks orange juice</u>_____.

2. (Chantavong   eat cereal)

    _____.

3. (I   drink orange juice with lunch)

    _____.

4. (Alma   have eggs for breakfast)

    _____.

5. (Oscar   have eggs for breakfast)

    _____.

6. (Howard   eat muffins)

    _____.

C. Rewrite these sentences using an adverb of frequency. Look at the box on page 53.

1. I eat beans every day _____ <u>I always eat beans.</u>_____

2. Lee drives to work only once a year._____.

3. Phong doesn't wash dishes._____.

4. Clara feeds the baby most of the time._____.

Unit 7   Grammar Check 7.3   **Future with *going to***

There are two ways to talk about future actions.

One way is to use the word **will**.

> I **will** see you tomorrow.

The other way is to use the verb **be** + **going to**.

I **am going** to leave in ten minutes.

I	**am going to**	study Italian next year.
You	**are going to**	leave soon.
He	**is going to**	cook dinner tonight.
She	**is going to**	buy a new car tomorrow.
It (the cat)	**is going to**	have babies.
We	**are going to**	have a party Friday night.
They	**are going to**	go home in half an hour.

A.   Write the future form in the blanks.

1.   You __are going to__ see a movie now, right?

2.   I _____ go to the post office after school.

3.   Kham and Viet _____ open a restaurant.

4.   The baby _____ sleep for six hours.

5.   The baby's mother _____ do some housework.

6.   You and I _____ bake bread this afternoon.

7.   Mrs. Rivera _____ be busy this evening.

8.   My family _____ give a big party Sunday afternoon.

B.   Answer these questions using the verb be + *going to.*

1.   What are you going to do tonight?

   <u>I am going to watch TV</u>_____.

2.   What is your mother going to do tomorrow morning?

   _____.

3.   What are your friends going to do on Saturday?

   _____.

4.   What are you going to do this afternoon?

   _____.

C.   Read each sentence. Then write another sentence using
   going to. **Use the words in parentheses in your new**
   sentence.

1.   Mexico is a beautiful country.   (Mr. and Mrs. Cato / visit Mexico)

   <u>Mr. and Mrs. Cato are going to visit Mexico</u>_____.

2.   It is a sunny day today.   (Amy / wear sunglasses)

   _____.

3.   I'm hungry.   (I / have some yogurt)

   _____.

4.   All his clothes are dirty.   (Pedro / do the laundry)

   _____.

5.   This concert is very long.   (You and I / leave soon)

   _____.

6.   Mrs. Rivera is going to bed.   (She / brush her teeth first)

   _____.

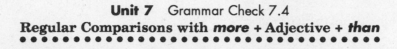

Unit 7 Grammar Check 7.4
Regular Comparisons with *more* + Adjective + *than*
• •

In Grammar Check 3.2 you saw some comparative adjectives that use *-er than* to compare two people, places, or things.

Alma is taller *than* Amos.

New York is larger *than* Boston.

My son is older *than* your son.

You use *-er than* when the adjective has only one syllable.

You use the pattern *more* + adjective + *than* when the adjective has three or more syllables.

A house is *more expensive than* an apartment.

Chinese is *more difficult than* Spanish.

A.   Circle the correct answer.

1.   Milk is (more cheap than / cheaper than) orange juice.

2.   Meat is (more expensive than / expensiver than) bread.

3.   Andres is (more young than / younger than) Carlos.

4.   Carlos is (more serious than / seriouser than) Andres.

5.   Carmen is (more strong than / stronger than) Lydia.

6.   Lydia is (more popular than / populerer than) Carmen.

7.   Ana is (more excited than / exciteder than) Jose.

8.   What subject is (more important than / importanter than) science?

B.   Look at the chart. Then write sentences using adjective + -er or more + adjective + than.

Name	Age	Serious?	Athletic?
Emi	10 years old	not serious	very athletic
Jun	8 years old	very serious	a little bit athletic
Fuji	6 years old	a little bit serious	a little bit athletic
Toshi	4 years old	very serious	not athletic

1.   (Jun / Emi / serious)
     <u>Jun is more serious than Emi</u>   .

2.   (Toshi / Jun / young)
     <u>Toshi is younger than Jun</u>   .

3.   (Fuji / Toshi / athletic)
     _____.

4.   (Toshi / Fuji / serious)
     _____.

5.   (Toshi / Emi serious)
     _____.

6.   (Fuji / Toshi / old)
     _____.

7.   (Emi / Fuji / athletic)
     _____.

8.   (Emi / Jun / athletic)
     _____.

9.   (Jun / Fuji / serious)
     _____.

Unit 7   Grammar Check 7.5   Irregular Comparative Adjectives

In Grammar Check 3.2 you used **-er than** to compare two people or things. For example: Maria is young**er than** Ana.

In Grammar Check 3.2 you also used **the ... -est** to compare more than two people or things: New York is **the largest** city in the U.S.

In Grammar Check 7.4 you used **more** + adjective + **than** with adjectives having three or more syllables: Roses are **more beautiful than** daisies.

Some adjectives don't follow these rules. Here is a list of some irregular adjectives.

Adjective	Comparative Adjective	Superlative Adjective
bad	worse	the worst
good	better	the best
a lot of	more	the most

Use this chart to do exercises A. and B. on page 60.

	They all have problems.	They all had a test.	They all have some money.
Gloria	the biggest problem of all	80%	$25
Julio	a very small problem	97%	$100
Trang	a small problem	90%	$75
Hans	a very big problem	60%	$10

A. Look at the chart on page 59. Circle the correct answer in each sentence.

1. Gloria has ((the worst problem) / the most money).

2. Trang has (a bad problem / a worse problem) than Julio.

3. Trang got (a good mark / the best mark) on the test.

4. Julio got (a bad mark / the best mark) on the test.

5. Gloria got (a better mark / a worse mark) than Trang.

6. Julio has (more money than Trang / the most money).

B. Look at the chart on page 59. Write the correct adjective in each blank. Use the words after each number.

1. (a lot of / more / (the most))
   Julio has ___the most___ money of all.

2. (a lot of / more / the most)
   Trang has _____ money than Gloria.

3. (a good / a better / the best)
   Trang got _____ mark than Hans.

4. (a bad / a worse / the worst)
   Hans got _____ mark of all.

5. (a lot of / more / the most)
   Trang has _____ money than Hans.

6. (a bad / a worse / the worst)
   Hans has _____ problem than Trang.

7. (a lot of / more / the most)
   Gloria has _____ money than Hans.

8. (a good / a better / the best)
   Gloria got _____ mark than Hans.

Answer Key

7.1

A. 1. libraries, 2. faces, 3. cities, 4. parties, 5. pharmacies, 6. babies, 7. boxes, 8. secretaries

B. 1. lady/ladies, 2. pharmacy/pharmacies, 3. secretary/secretaries, 4. city/cities, 5. french fry/french fries

C. 1. boxes, 2. kisses, 3. turkeys, 4. flies, 5. classes, 6. libraries, 7. boys, 8. babies, 9. glasses, 10. fruits, 11. stories, 12. dashes, 13. cities, 14. pencils, 15. sandwiches, 16. parties, 17. chimneys, 18. churches

7.2

A. 1. always, 2. sometimes, 3. rarely, 4. never, 5. usually, 6. usually, 7. never

B. 1. Delia sometimes drinks orange juice. 2. Chantavong rarely eats cereal. 3. I always drink orange juice with lunch. 4. Alma usually has eggs for breakfast. 5. Oscar never has eggs for breakfast. 6. Howard usually eats muffins.

C. 1. I always eat beans. 2. Lee rarely drives to work. 3. Phong never washes dishes. 4. Clara usually feeds the baby.

7.3

A. 1. are going to, 2. am going to, 3. are going to, 4. is going to, 5. is going to, 6. are going to, 7. is going to, 8. is going to (Other answers are possible)

B. 1. I am going to watch TV. 2. She is going to go to school. 3. They are going to go to the supermarket. 4. I am going to see a movie. (Other answers are possible.)

C. 1. Mr. and Mrs. Cato are going to visit Mexico. 2. Amy is going to wear sunglasses. 3. I am going to have some yogurt. 4. Pedro is going to do the laundry. 5. You and I are going to leave soon. 6. She is going to brush her teeth first.

7.4

A. 1. cheaper than, 2. more expensive than, 3. younger than, 4. more serious than, 5. stronger than, 6. more popular than, 7. more excited than, 8. more important than

B. 1. Jun is more serious than Emi. 2. Toshi is younger than Jun. 3. Fuji is more athletic than Toshi. 4. Toshi is more serious than Fuji. 5. Toshi is more serious than Emi. 6. Fuji is older than Toshi. 7. Emi is more athletic than Fuji. 8. Emi is more athletic than Jun. 9. Jun is more serious than Fuji.

7.5

A. 1. the worst problem, 2. a worse problem, 3. a good mark, 4. the best mark, 5. a worse mark, 6. the most money

B. 1. the most, 2. more, 3. a better, 4. the worst, 5. more, 6. a worse, 7. more, 8. a better

Unit 8

UNIT
8

Unit 8   Grammar Check 8.1
Questions with *How often...?*

In Grammar Check 7.2 you made statements using adverbs of frequency (***always, usually, sometimes, rarely,*** and ***never***). Adverbs of frequency are often used to answer **how often** questions.

Questions with **how often** are like the questions with **where** that you saw in Grammar Check 5.3 **How often** questions also use the helping verbs **do** and **does** and the simple form of the main verb.

How often	**do** or **does**	Noun	Simple form of verb	
How often	**do**	I	**come**	here?
How often	**do**	you	**wash**	the floor?
How often	**does**	he	**cook**	dinner?
How often	**does**	she	**visit**	her brother?
How often	**does**	it	**eat**?	
How often	**do**	we	**study**?	
How often	**do**	they	**buy**	food?

A.   Unscramble these sentences.

1. here   come   often   you   how   do

   <u>How often do you come here</u>_____?

2. often   she   laundry   does   do   how   the

   _____?

3. study   library   often   they   how   do   in   the

   _____?

4. the children TV often how the watch do

   _____?

5. Carlos bus often take does how the

   _____?

6. how deposit bank money often you do in the

   _____?

B. Look at the answers below. Then write questions using *how often*.

1. Question: <u>How often do they go to the movies</u>?
   Answer: They always go to the movies on Friday night.

2. Question: _____?
   Answer: Maria never speaks English at home.

3. Question: _____?
   Answer: I always answer the telephone.

4. Question: _____?
   Answer: Ali rarely eats meat.

5. Question: _____?
   Answer: My brother gets a haircut every month.

6. Question: _____?
   Answer: We have class two evenings a week.

7. Question: _____?
   Answer: I sometimes have coffee with breakfast.

8. Question: _____?
   Answer: My aunt usually visits her mother once a week.

Unit 8   Grammar Check 8.2
Statements with the Modal *should*
● ●

You use the word ***should*** to give people advice. ***Should*** shows that you think something is a good idea. ***Should*** is followed by the simple form of the verb.

Noun	Should	Simple Form of the verb	
I	***should***	***go***	now.
You	***should***	***see***	a dentist.
He	***should***	***go***	to bed.
She	***should***	***save***	some money.
We	***should***	***study***.	
They	***should***	***get***	a bigger apartment.

A.   Match the problem with the suggestion.

1. My car is 10 years old.   You should clean up.

    I have a stomachache.   You should stop eating.

    My sister is coming over tonight.   You should get a new one.

2. Rosa can't see the blackboard.   She should stand up.

    She has only $50 in the bank.   She should open the window.

    She is too warm.   She should save more money.

3. Jose and Eva are confused.   They should ask questions.

    They are too fat.   They should call him.

    They miss their grandfather.   They should eat less.

4. Luis has long hair.   He should eat more.

    He is very thin.   He should go out more often.

    He studies too much.   He should cut it.

5. It is raining.   He should wear glasses.

    He is very tired.   He should stop working.

    He can't see well.   He should wear a raincoat.

6. My floor is dirty.   You should take care of it.

    There is garbage on the floor.   You should throw it out.

    The baby is crying.   You should wash it.

B. Use the phrases in the box to make suggestions. Use each word only once.

study	get	make
take	put	save

1. Steak costs $8 a pound this week.

    <u>You should make</u> _____ fish for dinner.

2. I have a headache.

    _____ an aspirin.

3. Ali spends all his money.

    _____ some money in the bank.

4. Mr. and Mrs. Medina don't have medical insurance.

    _____ it.

5. Keisha wants to visit her family in Ghana.

    _____ her money.

6. I got a 50% score on my last test.

    _____ more.

Unit 8 Grammar Check 8.3 **Adjectives with -ed Endings**

In Grammar Check 3.2 you saw that adjectives describe people, places, things, and ideas.

Marika is a **tall** woman.	She's **tall**.
Miami is a **big** city.	It's **big**.
The rose is a **pretty** flower.	It's **pretty**.

Some English adjectives end in **-ed**. These adjectives come from verb forms.

Math confuses me.

I am confus**ed** in math class.

Going to a party excites me.

I am excit**ed** when I go to a party.

Some **-ed** Adjectives

excited	=	feeling very happy
depressed	=	feeling very unhappy
interested	=	want to know what is happening
bored	=	not interested in what is happening

A.   Circle the correct answer

1.   My English test score is 100%

I am (excited / bored).

2.   I have no money in my pocket.

I am (excited / depressed).

3.   I have read this lesson five times.

Now I am (bored / excited).

4.   Tell me more!

I am very (depressed / interested).

B.   **Write a sentence or two about each picture. Use the** *-ed*
adjectives in the box.

worried	=	thinking something bad is going to happen
bored	=	not interested in what is happening
interested	=	wanting to know what is happening
embarrassed	=	not wanting people to see what is happening to you
surprised	=	feeling confused when something happens
excited	=	feeling very happy

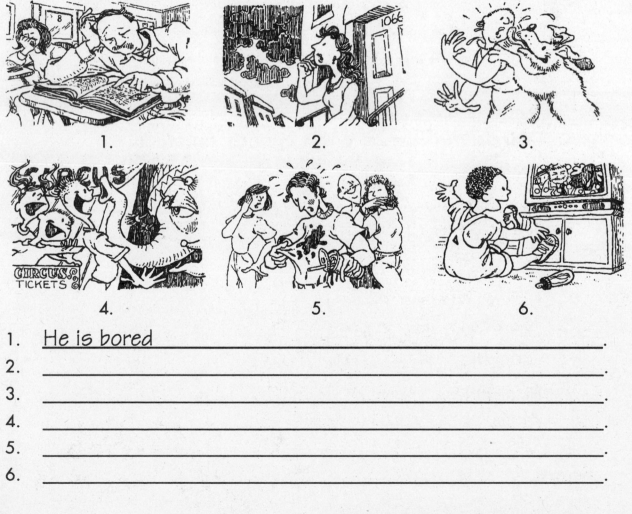

1.   2.   3.

4.   5.   6.

1. <u>He is bored</u> _____.
2. _____.
3. _____.
4. _____.
5. _____.
6. _____.

Unit 8   Grammar Check 8.4   Adverbs

Adverbs describe the actions of verbs.

Most adverbs end in **-ly**. (slowly) You will see them in Grammar Check 9.4.

Many adverbs are related to adjectives (slow/slowly).

Some words can be both adjectives and adverbs. They do not end in **-ly**. Some examples are **hard, fast, early,** and **late**.

Adjective Uses	**Adverb Uses**
This test is **hard**.	I work **hard**.
It's a **fast** car.	She drives **fast**.
I get an **early** bus.	I always leave **early**.
Take the **late** train.	The 3:00 train always arrives **late**.

A.   Circle the correct word in each sentence.

1. The train is (lately / (late)).

2. Eric talks (fastly / fast).

3. This book is (hard / hardly).

4. I woke up (lately / early).

5. I can run very (fast / early).

6. I finish work (early / hard).

7. I always leave the house (late / hard).

8. He reads (fast / hard).

9. He tries (early / hard).

10. Can you stay (early / late)?

B. Unscramble these sentences.

1. hard   test   Mario   for   the   studies

    <u>Mario studies hard for the test</u>   .

2. language   is   hard   me   Chinese   a   for

    _____ .

3. house   fast   Kim   very   cleans   the

    _____ .

4. reader   Aslan   very   is   fast   a

    _____ .

5. late   every   works   Mrs. Lee   night

    _____ .

6. late   bus   is   the   today

    _____ .

C. In front of each question, write the letter of the correct answer.

<u> C </u> 1. Why are you running?   a. Yes, I can.

____ 2. Why are you so tired?   b. No, but I try hard.

____ 3. Does your sister get up early?   c. My bus is late.

____ 4. Can you run fast?   d. Yes, it is.

____ 5. Is your bus late?   e. I'm working very hard.

____ 6. Do you do well on your tests?   f. I like getting up early.

____ 7. Why do you get up at 5:00?   g. Yes, she does.

____ 8. Why are the students angry?   h. The teacher is late for class.

8.1

A. 1. How often do you come here? 2. How often does she do the laundry? 3. How often do they study in the library? 4. How often do the children watch TV? 5. How often does Carlos take the bus? 6. How often do you deposit money in the bank?

B. 1. How often do they go to the movies? 2. How often does Maria speak English at home? 3. How often do you answer the telephone? 4. How often does Ali eat meat? 5. How often does your brother get a haircut? 6. How often do we have class? 7. How often do you have coffee with breakfast? 8. How often does your aunt visit her mother?

8.2

A. 1. old—You should get, stomachache—You should stop, tonight—You should clean, 2. blackboard—She should stand, bank—She should save, warm—She should open, 3. confused—They should ask, fat—They should eat, grandfather—They should call, 4. hair—He should cut, thin—He should eat, much—He should go out, 5. raining—he should wear a raincoat, tired—he should stop, well—He should wear glasses, 6. dirty—You should wash, floor—You should throw, crying—You should take care

B. 1. You should make, 2. You should take, 3. He should put, 4. They should get, 5. She should save, 6. You should study

8.3

A. 1. excited, 2. depressed, 3. bored, 4. interested

B. 1. He is bored. 2. She is worried. 3. She is surprised. 4. They are excited. 5. He is embarrassed. 6. He is interested. (Other answers are possible.)

8.4

A. 1. late, 2. fast, 3. hard, 4. early, 5. fast, 6. early, 7. late, 8. fast, 9. hard, 10. late

B. 1. Mario studies hard for the test. 2. Chinese is a hard language for me. 3. Kim cleans the house very fast. 4. Aslan is a very fast reader. 5. Mrs. Lee works late every night. 6. The bus is late today.

C. 1. c, 2. e, 3. g, 4. a, 5. d, 6. b, 7. f, 8. h

Unit 9

U N I T
9

Unit 9 Grammar Check 9.1
Past Tense Questions and Statements, Regular Verbs
● ●

Use the past tense to talk about actions that happened in the past.

Use **did** + the simple form of the verb to ask past tense questions.

Add **-ed** to the simple form of regular verbs to make past tense statements.

What	**did**	you **want** for dinner?
I	want**ed**	soup for dinner.
How long	**did**	you **watch** TV last night?
We	watch**ed**	TV for three hours.

A. Look at the chart. Then fill in the blanks in each sentence.

Name	Activity	When?
Lena	cook dinner	last night
Jerry	listen to music	yesterday afternoon
Mr. Andrada	work hard	this morning
Phong	watch TV	Saturday morning
Lisa	play soccer	yesterday

1. What _____ did _____ Lena do _____ last night _____ ?

   She ____ cooked dinner ____ last night.

2. What _____ Jerry do _____ ?

   He _____ yesterday afternoon.

3. What _____ Mr. Andrada do _____ ?

   He _____ this morning.

4. What _____ Phong do _____ ?

   He _____ Saturday morning.

5. What _____ Lisa do _____ ?

   She _____ yesterday.

B. Write past tense questions and answers.

1. (what / you / last night)   (talk on the phone / all evening)

   <u>What did you do last night</u> _____?

   <u>I talked on the phone all evening</u> _____.

2. (how long / Alice / play cards)   (for three hours)

   _____?

   _____.

3. (what / they / this morning)   (listen to music)

   _____?

   _____.

4. (how long / you / work / yesterday)   (all day)

   _____?

   _____.

5. (what / Eric / last week)   (visit / his brother / in Texas)

   _____?

   _____.

Unit 9 Grammar Check 9.2
Past Tense Questions and Short Answers with *to be*
• •

Use **was** and **were** to ask yes/no questions.

Use **was** (**wasn't**) and **were** (**weren't**) to answer yes/no questions.

Questions	**Answers**	
Was I late?	Yes, you **were**.	No, you **weren't**.
Were you a teacher?	Yes, I **was**.	No, I **wasn't**.
Was he a farmer?	Yes, he **was**.	No, he **wasn't**.
Was she a doctor?	Yes, she **was**.	No, she **wasn't**.
Was it a good job?	Yes, it **was**.	No, it **wasn't**.
Were we good students?	Yes, we **were**.	No, we **weren't**.
Were they nurses?	Yes, they **were**.	No, they **weren't**.

A. Match the questions with the answers.

1. Was Maria a homemaker?   No, they weren't.
    Was I early?   Yes, you were.
    Were Ali and Rita late again?   Yes, she was.

2. Were you a government worker?   No, he wasn't.
    Were the children very young?   No, I wasn't.
    Was John married?   Yes, they were.

3. Was Linus a bartender?   Yes, I was.
    Was Alice a cook?   No, she wasn't.
    Were you happy?   Yes, he was.

B. Look at the box on page 71. Then complete the short answers below.

1. Were you early?   Yes, __I was__ .

2. Was Pedro a mechanic?   No, _____ .

3. Was Sara busy yesterday?   Yes, _____ .

4. Were we good students?   No, _____ .

5. Was I late?   Yes, _____ .

6. Were you a fast worker?   No, _____ .

7. Was it late?   Yes, _____ .

8. Was I a nurse?   No, _____ .

9. Was she a soldier?   Yes, _____ .

10. Were they in business?   No, _____ .

C. Write questions and answers in the past tense.

1. (Alexi / late to class)   __Was Alexi late to class__ ?

    (Yes)   __Yes, he was__ .

2. (they / hard workers)   _____ ?

    (No)   _____ .

3. (you and I / late)   _____ ?

    (Yes)   _____ .

4. (I / a singer)   _____ ?

    (No)   _____ .

5. (you / a waiter)   _____ ?

    (Yes)   _____ .

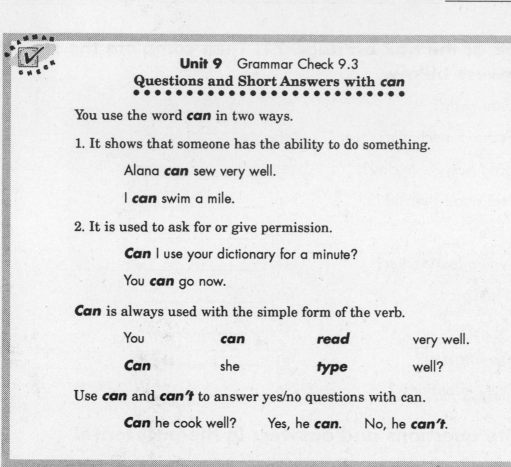

Unit 9 Grammar Check 9.3
Questions and Short Answers with *can*

You use the word ***can*** in two ways.

1. It shows that someone has the ability to do something.

Alana ***can*** sew very well.

I ***can*** swim a mile.

2. It is used to ask for or give permission.

Can I use your dictionary for a minute?

You ***can*** go now.

Can is always used with the simple form of the verb.

| You | ***can*** | ***read*** | very well. |
| ***Can*** | she | ***type*** | well? |

Use ***can*** and ***can't*** to answer yes/no questions with can.

Can he cook well?   Yes, he ***can***.   No, he ***can't***.

A. Match the pairs of sentences.

1. Maria has a beautiful voice.   She can't sing at all.
    Alma has a bad voice.   She can't sing right now.
    My sister is very tired today.   She can sing very well.

2. I can cut hair very well.   I am a barber.
    I can't fix cars.   I can't use a computer.
    I don't know how to type at all.   I need to find a mechanic.

3. Richard can sew.   He can make his own clothes.
    Bill can't drive.   He should take the bus.
    Alan needs a plumber.   He can't fix the pipes.

B. **Make sentences using** *can* **or** *can't.* **Use the words after each number.**

1. (I / sing very well)
   <u>I can (can't) sing very well.</u>

2. (I / speak Chinese)
   _____.

3. (my English teacher / speak my native language)
   _____.

4. (my classmates / understand me)
   _____.

5. (my sister / type)
   _____.

6. (my living room / hold 15 people)
   _____.

7. (I / study late at night)
   _____.

8. (my best friend / play tennis)
   _____.

C. **Answer each question with a short answer.**

1. Can you speak French?   <u>Yes, I can. (No, I can't)</u>.

2. Can a baby ride a bicycle?   _____.

3. Can a woman be a baseball player? _____.

4. Can you play the piano well?   _____.

5. Can a fish climb a tree?   _____.

6. Can a dog swim?   _____.

Unit 9   Grammar Check 9.4   **Adverbs with -ly**

Adverbs describe the actions of verbs.

In Grammar Check 8.4 you saw some adverbs that do not end in **-ly**.

She is working **hard**.

He writes very **fast**.

I like to arrive **early**.

She always leaves **late**.

However, most adverbs do end in **-ly**.

Many adverbs are related to adjectives.

That man is slow.
(**Slow** is an adjective that describes **that man**.)

He drives slowly.
(**Slowly** is an adverb that describes **how the man drives**.)

Sample Adjectives   Sample Adverbs

slow   **slowly**

quick   **quickly**

loud   **loudly**

A.   Circle the correct word.

1.   Mario is a ((slow) / slowly) runner.

He runs (slow / (slowly)).

2.   This computer is very (quick / quickly).

It prints out the pages very (quick / quickly).

3.   Eva has a (loud / loudly) voice.

She sings (loud / loudly).

4. Mountain climbing can be a (dangerous / dangerously) sport.

I like living (dangerous / dangerously).

5. Your garden is (beautiful / beautifully).

The flowers grow (beautiful / beautifully).

6. José speaks very (clear / clearly).

He has a (clear / clearly) voice.

B.   Circle the adjective in each sentence. Then rewrite the sentence using a related adverb.

1. Carmen has a very (soft) voice.

She speaks softly _____.

2. Carlos is a careful driver.

_____.

3. Bill is a slow runner.

_____.

4. He is a calm listener.

_____.

5. Manuel is a very neat painter.

_____.

6. Eva is a clear speaker.

_____.

7. Anton is a quick learner.

_____.

8. I have a loud voice.

_____.

Unit 9 Grammar Check 9.5
Future Tense Questions and Answers with *will*
• •

In Grammar Check 7.3 you saw one way to talk about future events.

I ***am going to*** leave in ten minutes.

Lucia ***is going to*** visit her uncle next week.

The other way is to use the word ***will***. The statements and questions use ***will*** or ***won't (will not)*** + the simple form of the main verb.

I ***will go*** alone.   I ***won't go*** alone.

Will you ***go*** alone?

Short answers use ***will*** and ***won't***.

Yes, I ***will***.   No, I ***won't***.

A.   Write *will* or *won't* in each blank.

1.   I don't like restaurant food.

I ____will____ eat at home.

2.   I love horror movies.

I _____ see *Dracula Dies*.

3.   I am taking a vacation next week.

Where _____ you go?

4.   Chan is going to the movies tonight.

She _____ be home all evening.

5. Maria is taking the bus.

She _____ drive her car.

6. We're going away for the weekend.

We _____ be home Sunday night.

B.   Answer the following questions. Use short answers.

1. Will you be in school on Friday?   <u>Yes, I will</u>   .

2. Will the teacher teach another class today?   _____.

3. Will your brother call you on your birthday?   _____.

4. Will you take the bus home tonight?   _____.

5. Will your classmates eat lunch at school?   _____.

6. Will it rain today?   _____.

C.   Read each sentence. Then rewrite it using *will* **or** *won't*.

1. The doctor is going to examine a patient.

    <u>The doctor will examine a patient</u>   .

2. The patient is going to get an expensive prescription.

    _____.

3. The patient isn't going to be happy.

    _____.

4. The pharmacist is going to charge $42.00 for the medicine.

    _____.

5. The patient is going to feel better fast.

    _____.

6. The patient is going to thank the doctor.

    _____.

9.1

A. 1. did/last night/cooked dinner, 2. did/yesterday afternoon/listened to music, 3. did/this morning/worked hard, 4. did/Saturday morning/watched TV, 5. did/yesterday/played soccer

B. 1. What did you do last night? I talked on the phone all evening. 2. How long did Alice play cards? She played cards for three hours. 3. What did they do this morning? They listened to music this morning. 4. How long did you work yesterday? I worked all day yesterday. 5. What did Eric do last week? He visited his brother in Texas.

9.2

A. 1. homemaker?—Yes, she, early?—Yes, you, again?—No, they, 2. worker?—No, I, young?—Yes, they, married?—No, he, 3. bartender?—Yes, he, cook?—No she, happy?—Yes, I

B. 1. I was, 2. he wasn't, 3. she was, 4. we weren't, 5. you were, 6. I wasn't, 7. it was, 8. you weren't, 9. she was, 10. they weren't

C. 1. Was Alexi late to class? Yes, he was. 2. Were they hard workers? No, they weren't. 3. Were you and I late? Yes, we were. 4. Was I a singer? No, you weren't. 5. Were you a waiter? Yes, I was.

9.3

1. beautiful voice—She can sing, bad voice—She can't sing at all, tired today—She can't sing right now, 2. well—I am a barber, cars—I need to find, type at all—I can't use, 3. sew—He can make, drive—He should take, plumber—He can't fix

B. 1. I can (can't) sing very well. 2. I can (can't) speak Chinese. 3. My English teacher can (can't) speak my native language. 4. My classmates can (can't) understand me. 5. My sister can (can't) type. 6. My living room can (can't) hold 15 people. 7. I can (can't) study late at night. 8. My best friend can (can't) play tennis.

C. 1. Yes, I can. (No, I can't.) 2. No, it can't. 3. Yes, she can. 4. Yes, I can. (No, I can't.) 5. No, it can't. 6. Yes, it can.

9.4

A. 1. slow/slowly, 2. quick/quickly, 3. loud/loudly, 4. dangerous/dangerously, 5. beautiful/beautifully, 6. clearly/clear

B. 1. She speaks softly. 2. He drives carefully. 3. He runs slowly. 4. He listens calmly. 5. He paints neatly. 6. She speaks clearly. 7. He learns quickly. 8. I talk loudly.

9.5

A. 1. will, 2. will, 3. will, 4. won't, 5. won't, 6. will (won't)

B. 1. Yes, I will. 2. Yes, he/she will. (No, he/she won't.) 3. Yes, he will. (No, he won't.) 4. Yes, I will. (No, I won't.) 5. Yes, they will. (No, they won't.) 6. Yes, it will. (No, it won't.)

C. 1. The doctor will examine a patient. 2. The patient will get an expensive prescription. 3. The patient won't be happy. 4. The pharmacist will charge $42.00 for the medicine. 5. The patient will feel better fast. 6. The patient will thank the doctor.

Unit 10

UNIT
10

Unit 10   Grammar Check 10.1   *Like to* + Verb

Use *like to* + the simple form of the verb to talk about something you enjoy doing.

> I *like to go* to bed early.   (every night)

> I *like to get* to class early.   (every day)

You use *do, does, don't,* and *doesn't* in questions and short answers with *like to*.

> **Do**   you   like to swim?

> Yes, I **do**.   No, I **don't**.

A.   Match each item in Column A with an item in Column B.

Column A	Column B

1. I always get up early — so I joined the YMCA.

I like to shop for clothes — because I don't like to sleep late.

I like to swim — when I have money.

2. Ella doesn't like to play soccer — so she moved to the country.

Ella likes to paint — because she is too slow.

Ella likes to work in the garden — and she makes great pictures.

3. We like to sing — and we have a great camera.

We like to take pictures — but they cost too much.

We like visiting museums — so we bought a piano.

B.   Write questions and answers with *like to.*

1.   (you / play chess / with your brother)   (no)
   <u>Do you like to play chess with your brother</u>   ?
   <u>No, I don't</u>   .

2.   (Roberto / listen to salsa music)   (yes)
   _____?
   _____.

3.   (Julia / cook dinner for her family)   (no)
   _____?
   _____.

4.   (they / take care of children)   (yes)
   _____?
   _____.

5.   (we / take tests)   (no)
   _____?
   _____.

C.   Rewrite these sentences using the words *like to* **or** *likes to.*

1.   Esin doesn't enjoy doing the laundry.
   <u>Esin doesn't like to do the laundry</u>   .

2.   Peter enjoys going fishing.
   _____.

3.   I love watching TV.
   _____.

4.   Ellie and Steve think skiing is fun.
   _____.

Unit 10 Grammar Check 10.2
Some Irregular Past Tense Verbs
• • • • • • • • • • • • • • • • • • • •

In Grammar Check 9.1 you used the past tense to talk about actions that happened in the past. You added **-ed** to the simple form to make past tense statements.

You do not add **-ed** to some verbs to form the past tense. These verbs have special past tense forms. They are called irregular verbs.

Where did you	**go**	last night?
I	**went**	to a movie.
What did you	**have**	for dinner?
I	**had**	pizza.

A. Write a past tense verb in each blank. Use the words in the box.

Base Form	Past Tense	Base Form	Past Tense
come	came	have	had
do	did	ride	rode
go	went	say	said

1. Where did you go to high school?

    I ____went____ to high school in Haiti.

2. When did you have your first child?

    I _____ my first child in 1990.

3. When did you come to this country?

    I _____ here in 1995.

4. What did you do before class today?

    I _____ my homework.

5. Did you go to the doctor yesterday?

   Yes, I _____ to the doctor yesterday.

6. What did the doctor say?

   He _____ I was OK.

B. Write past tense questions and answers. Look at the words in the box on page 81.

1. (where / Alex / have dinner / last night)   (at home)

   <u>Where did Alex have dinner last night</u> _____?

   <u>He had dinner at home</u> _____.

2. (when / you / ride / your bicycle)   (after school)

   _____?

   _____.

3. (when / she / do the laundry)   (on Saturday)

   _____?

   _____.

4. (what time / we / go home / last night)   (at 11:00)

   _____?

   _____.

5. (when / the teacher / come in)   (a minute ago)

   _____?

   _____.

6. (what / she / say)   (hello)

   _____?

   _____.

Unit 10 Grammar Check 10.3 **When** Clauses
• •

You use a **when** clause to show that two things happen at the same time. These events can be in the past, in the present, or in the future.

The weather was cold	**when** I arrived here.
They feel happy	**when** they sing.
She will get a job	**when** she finishes school.

When clauses have three parts.

	When ⇩	subject ⇩	verb ⇩
(I will say good-bye)	when	I	leave.
(What did he do)	when	he	arrived?

A. Match each item in Column A with an item in Column B.

Column A   Column B

1. How did he feel   when it saw me.
    The dog jumped   when you came in.
    You looked happy   when he failed the test?

2. They are happy   when they play soccer.
    They feel sad   when they say goodbye.
    They get excited   when they sing.

3. She eats   when she has a test.
    She sleeps   when she is hungry.
    She studies   when she is tired.

B. **Write questions and answers with** *when* **clauses. Use the present tense in all answers.**

1. (what / she / do / when / happy)   (sing)
    <u>What does she do when she is happy</u>   ?
    <u>She sings when she is happy</u>   .

2. (where / you / go / when / hungry)   (a restaurant)
    _____   ?
    _____   .

3. (what / Larry / do / when / leave school)   (go home)
    _____   ?
    _____   .

4. (where / we / eat / when / have no money)   (at home)
    _____   ?
    _____   .

5. (who / we / visit / when / have time)   (our grandparents)
    _____   ?
    _____   .

6. (what / you / do / when / nervous)   (take a deep breath)
    _____   ?
    _____   .

7. (what / he / drink / when / thirsty)   (water)
    _____   ?
    _____   .

8. (when / the teacher / leave school)   (class is over)
    _____   ?
    _____   .

Unit 10 Grammar Check 10.4
Questions, Short Answers, and Statements with *would like to*

In Grammar Check 10.1 you saw that sentences with **like to** plus the simple form of the verb describe activities that are enjoyable.

I **like to watch** TV.   (every night)

I **like to eat** a big breakfast.   (every day)

When you use **would like to** + the simple form of the verb, you show that you want to do something now or in the future.

I **would like to buy** an expensive car.   (someday)

I **would like to visit** San Francisco.   (if I can)

You use **would** and **wouldn't** in questions and short answers with **like to**.

Would you like to watch TV?

Yes, I **would**.   No, I **wouldn't**.

A. Match each item in Column A with an item in Column B.

Column A	Column B
1. I would like to study Spanish	when I finish school.
I would like to open a bank account	before I visit Mexico.
I would like to get a better job	when I earn some money.
2. Carlos would like to buy a car,	but the neighbors are too noisy.
Carlos would like to get more sleep,	but he doesn't have the money.
Carlos would like to give a party,	but he's too busy.
3. We would like to have a dog,	but our apartment is too small.
We would like to travel,	but we don't have the time.
We would like to go swimming,	but the weather is too cold.

Name _____ Date _____

B.   Write questions and answers with *would like to.*

1.   (you / have some pizza)   (no)

_Would you like to have some pizza_____?

_No, I wouldn't_____._

2.   (Rita / go to college)   (yes)

_____?

_____.

3.   (Phoumy / have his own business)   (no)

_____?

_____.

4.   (they / be rich and famous)   (yes)

_____?

_____.

C.   Rewrite these sentences using the words *would like to.*

1.   We want to go skiing next winter.

_We would like to go skiing next winter._____

2.   Marta plans to become an American citizen if she can.

_____.

3.   I want to buy a 26-inch TV.

_____.

4.   Sue and Sam plan to get married next summer.

_____.

10.1

A. 1. early—because, clothes—when, swim—so, 2. soccer—because, paint—and, garden—so, 3. sing—so, pictures—and, museums—but

B. 1. Do you like to play chess with your brother? No, I don't. 2. Does Roberto like to listen to salsa music? Yes, he does. 3. Does Julia like to cook dinner for her family? No, she doesn't. 4. Do they like to take care of children? Yes, they do. 5. Do we like to take tests? No, we don't.

C. 1. Esin doesn't like to do the laundry. 2. Peter likes to go fishing. 3. I like to watch TV. 4. Ellie and Steve like to ski.

10.2

A. 1. went, 2. had, 3. came, 4. did, 5. went, 6. said

B. 1. Where did Alex have dinner last night? He had dinner at home. 2. When did you ride your bicycle? I rode my bicycle after school. 3. When did she do the laundry? She did the laundry on Saturday. 4. What time did we go home last night? We went home at 11:00. 5. When did the teacher come in? He/She came in a minute ago. 6. What did she say? She said hello.

10.3

A. 1. feel—when he failed, jumped—when it saw, happy—when you came, 2. happy—when they sing, sad—when they say goodbye, excited—when they play, 3. eats—when she is hungry, sleeps—when she is tired, studies—when she has a test.

B. 1. What does she do when she is happy? She sings when she is happy. 2. Where do you go when you are hungry? I go to a restaurant when I am hungry. 3. What does Larry do when he leaves school? Larry goes home when he leaves school. 4. Where do we eat when he have no money? We eat at home when we have no money. 5. Who do we visit when we have time? We visit our grandparents when we have time. 6. What do you do when you are nervous? I take a deep breath when I am nervous. 7. What does he drink when he's thirsty? He drinks water when he is thirsty. 8. When does the teacher leave school? He/She leaves school when class is over.

10.4

A. 1. Spanish—before I visit, account—when I earn, job—when I finish, 2. car—but he doesn't have, sleep—but the neighbors, party—but he's too busy, 3. dog—but our apartment, travel—but we don't have, swimming—but the weather

B. 1. Would you like to have some pizza? No, I wouldn't. 2. Would Rita like to go to college? Yes, she would. 3. Would Phoumy like to have his own business? No, he wouldn't. 4. Would they like to be rich and famous? Yes, they would.

C. 1. We would like to go skiing next winter. 2. Marta would like to become an American citizen if she can. 3. I would like to buy a 26-inch TV. 4. Sue and Sam would like to get married next summer.